STUDIES IN

ARABIC PHILOSOPHY

STUDIES IN

ARABIC PHILOSOPHY

by

NICHOLAS RESCHER

Professor of Philosophy in the University of Pittsburgh

UNIVERSITY OF PITTSBURGH PRESS

86909

Library of Congress Catalog Number: 67-18690

Printed in England by Stephen Austin & Sons, Ltd., Hertford

PREFACE

The present volume gathers together ten studies of various facets of Arabic philosophy and its influence upon the West. All in all, about half of the material presented here is making its appearance in print for the first time. Several of these studies have previously appeared in learned journals, and are reprinted here with only minor changes:

" Yaḥyā ibn 'Adī's Treatise on the Four Scientific Questions Regarding the Art of Logic," *Journal of the History of Ideas*, vol. 25 (1964), pp. 572–578. The translation of the Arabic text presented here was made in collaboration with Professor Fadlou Shehadi.

" Nicholas of Cusa on the Qur'ān," *The Muslim World*, vol. 55 (1965), pp. 195–202.

" The Impact of Arabic Philosophy on the West," *The Islamic Quarterly*, vol. 10 (1966), pp. 3–11.

" Avicenna on the Logic of Questions," *Archiv für Geschichte der Philosophie*, vol. 49 (1967), pp. 1–6.

Also, the first chapter incorporates the contents of a published article, " Al-Kindī's Epistle on the Concentric Structure of the Universe," *Isis*, vol. 56 (1965), pp. 190–195, which includes a translation of an Arabic text made in collaboration with Professor Haig Khatchadourian. And chapter VII draws heavily upon my monograph on *Temporal Modalities in Arabic Logic* (Dordrecht, D. Reidel, 1966). I am grateful to the various editors and publishers involved, and to my collaborators, for their permission to reprint this material.

I want to thank Miss Dorothy Henle for her conscientious help in preparing all this difficult material for publication and in compiling the Index, and Miss Alena Horner and Miss Judy Bazy for helping me to see the work through the press.

It also affords me great pleasure to record my sincere thanks to the National Science Foundation. Most of the papers brought together here are part of a series of studies of Arabic contributions to logic supported by a research grant from the Foundation.

Nicholas Rescher

Pittsburgh
December 1966

CONTENTS

STUDIES IN

ARABIC PHILOSOPHY

I

AL-KINDĪ'S EPISTLE
"ON THE CONCENTRIC STRUCTURE
OF THE UNIVERSE"

A. INTRODUCTION

1. Al-Kindī

Abū Yūsuf Yaʻqūb ibn Isḥāq al-Kindī, whose name was Latinized to Alkindus or Alkendus, was born around 805 in Kufah. Descended from a noble Arab tribe, the banū Kindah, he was the only Arabic philosopher of pure Arab descent, and was consequently dubbed " the philosopher of the Arabs."[1]

Little is known about al-Kindī's training and education.   His father—the governor of Kufah during the reigns of the caliphs al-Mahdī (reigned 775–785) and his son al-Rashīd (reigned 786–809)—died before 809, leaving al-Kindī orphaned, but endowed with wealth and a name of great prestige. As a child, al-Kindī lived at Basra, but during the reign of al-Maʼmūn (reigned 813–833) he removed to Baghdad, the Abbasid capital, to pursue his studies at this great center of learning. He must—somehow—have been under the influence of non-Islamic scholars, for these then possessed the monopoly on the Greek science and philosophy to which al-Kindī dedicated himself with great devotion.   His contacts with the

---

[1] For al-Kindī consult: N. Rescher, *Al-Kindī: An Annotated Bibliography* (Pittsburgh, 1964); Carl Brockelmann, *Geschichte der arabischen Litteratur*, vol. I (Weimar, 1898), pp. 209–210; vol. I (2d ed., Leiden, 1943), pp. 230–231; Supplementband I (Leiden, 1937), pp. 372–374; George Sarton, *Introduction to the History of Science*, vol. I (Baltimore, 1927), pp. 559–560; L. Massignon in *The Encyclopedia of Islam*, vol. II (1st ed., Leiden, 1913), p. 1021; F. Ueberweg and L. Geyer, *Grundriss der Geschichte der Philosophie*, vol. II (Berlin, 1928), pp. 303–304, 720.

Christian scholars of his place and time, some of whose Arabic translations of Greek work were sponsored by him, were extensive. (Al-Kindī is reported to have been a patron of various translators, several important scholars being identifiable among them: Ibn Nā'imah, Asṭāt (= ? Eustatius), and Yaḥyā ibn al-Biṭrīq.) However, al-Kindī's intellectual attitude toward Christianity was hostile —he even wrote a " Refutation of the Christians."

Throughout his adult life al-Kindī lived in Baghdad, then at the height of a vigorous flowering of artistic and intellectual culture— where he was closely connected with the courts of the caliphs al-Ma'mūn and al-Mu'taṣim during whose reigns the Abbasid caliphate reached great heights. He may well have been instrumental in the establishment or in the management of the *Bait al-ḥikmah*, the institute founded by al-Ma'mūn around 830 for the translation into Arabic of Greek philosophical and scientific work. Al-Kindī's own literary output was prodigious.[2] More than 350 treatises are ascribed to him, of which only some sixty to seventy appear to have survived.[3]

The caliph al-Mu'taṣim (reigned 833–842)—to whom al-Kindī dedicated his largest philosophical treatise, *Fī 'l-falsafah al-ūlā* (" On first philosophy ")—was impressed by al-Kindī's great learning and appointed him to an official position at his court (as court astronomer). It is reported that a keen hostility developed between al-Kindī and the banū Mūsā, the " sons of Moses," i.e., of Mūsā ibn Shākir (d. ca. 840), mathematicians, astronomers, and patrons of science, who were also favorites of al-Ma'mūn. The principal reason for this hostility was resentment that the caliph

---

[2] An excellent general survey of al-Kindī's scholarly activities is F. Rosenthal, " Al-Kindī als Literat," *Orientalia*, vol. 11 (1942), pp. 262–288. See also S. Hamarneh, " Al-Kindī, A Ninth-Century Physician, Philosopher, and Scholar," *Medical History*, vol. 9 (1965), pp. 328–342.

[3] For al-Kindī's writings see: Gustav Flügel, " Al-Kindī: Gennant ' Der Philosoph der Araber '," in *Abhandlungen für die Kunde des Morgenlandes*, vol. I (Marburg, 1857), pp. 1–54 (separately paginated); Albino Nagy, " Sulle opere di Ja'qūb ben Isḥāq al-Kindī," *Rendiconti della Reale Accademia dei Lincei* (classe di scienze morali, storiche e filologiche), vol. 4 (1895), pp. 157–170. The most recent and accurate listing of al-Kindī's writings is R. J. McCarthy, *Al-Taṣānīf mansūbat ilā failusūf al-'arab* (The Works Attributed to " The Philosopher of the Arabs " [= al-Kindī]) (Baghdad, 1963).

al-Mu'taṣim appointed al-Kindī, not one of the banū Mūsā, as tutor to his son Aḥmad.[4]

Unfortunately for al-Kindī, his cordial relationship with the Abbasid palace came to an end with the ascendancy of reactionary forces during the rule of al-Mutawakkil (reigned 847–861), who—in response to grave charges by the banū Mūsā—ordered the confiscation of al-Kindī's library. After 861, al-Kindī regained his books, thanks to his friendship with prince Aḥmad. He may also have regained some of his public prestige but did not recover his status at court.

After reaching a position of fame and wide repute, al-Kindī died in Baghdad around 870, probably in 873.

Whatever may have been the impetus to do so, the fact is that al-Kindī made a profound study of Greek learning, and made a great contribution to its establishment in the orbit of Islam, to some extent by his patronage of the work of others, but primarily through his own large and influential productivity. He was among the first Arabic scholars to interest himself in philosophy from a viewpoint centering around scientific rather than theological interests. Indeed, it would seem appropriate to regard al-Kindī as primarily a scientist or " *natural* " philosopher, rather than a " pure " one: his interest in pure philosophy seems to have been secondary and derivative, coming about largely because this was an integral part of the unified corpus of Greek philosophic-scientific knowledge accessible in his time and place.

2. *Al-Kindī's Concept of Scientific Method*

On al-Kindī's own view, he " considered it as his task to serve as an Arab transmitter and interpreter of the ancient heritage ,"[5]—as a modern authority put it. On this showing, al-Kindī set himself a definite, but distinctly limited goal: the projection of Greek learning into an Arabic setting. How did he go about the accomplishment of this mission, and what—if anything—did he himself contribute in the course of its discharge ? These are the main questions which will concern us here.

One noteworthy feature of al-Kindī, viewed in the perspective as a

[4] See J. Ruska in *Encyclopedia of Islam* (1st ed.), vol. III, p. 742 (English version).
[5] F. Rosenthal, " Al-Kindī and Ptolemy," *Studi Orientalistici*, vol. 2 (1956), p. 455.

3

proponent of Greek learning, is his marked avoidance of argumentation from authority as such. Very often, even when patently relying upon an eminent ancient authority such as Aristotle or Euclid or Ptolemy, al-Kindī presents his views without explicit attribution : the authority is *drawn upon*, but not *invoked*.[6] Al-Kindī looks to the Greek authorities for guidance, but places no reliance upon the " weight of authority " as such as a supporting argument for the correctness of views.

A particularly striking feature of al-Kindī's use of the Greek authorities is his eclecticism. In the manner of the neo-Pythagorean natural philosophers of his day, such as al-Razī and the banū Mūsā, al-Kindī drew indiscriminately on various Greek schools. Plato or Aristotle, the philosophers or the mathematicians, the rationalistic natural scientists or the neo-Pythagorean number-mystics, all provide grist to his mill. His purview is definitely not restricted to the confines of any sect, discipline, or school. Moreover, it is quite plain from the character of his reported and especially of his surviving writings, that, as present-day terminology goes, al-Kindī's interests are far more accurately characterized as being concerned with *scientific* rather than strictly *philosophical* subjects: his philosophy is pre-eminently *natural* philosophy.[7]

At bottom, al-Kindī was not a " scientist " in the sense in which we would nowadays understand the term, but a *scholar*—not one who by original observations penetrated the secrets of Nature, but one who from the writings of others extracted the ideas which formed the substance of his own writings. The foundation of his work was the library of the scholar, whose " data " are his books, rather than the observations of the physician, the alchemist, or the astronomer.[8]

---

[6] An interesting case-study in al-Kindī's use of ancient authorities in his exploitation of Ptolemy, for which see F. Rosenthal, *op. cit.*, and cf. *idem, Das Fortleben der Antike im Islam* (Zürich, 1965), pp. 293–303.

[7] See N. Rescher, *Al-Kindī: An Annotated Bibliography* (Pittsburgh, 1964), especially pp. 41–53.

[8] A possible exception to this generalization is al-Kindī's discussions of chemistry/alchemy. The principal item here is his treatise *Kīmiyā' al-'itr wa-'l-taṣ'īdat* (" The chemistry of perfume and distillation ") published by K. Garbers in 1948 (*Abhandlungen für die Kunde des Morgenlandes*, vol. 30; Leipzig, 1948). The author of this work reveals himself, in Garbers' words, as a " nüchtern denkender, auf Erfahrung fussender Praktiker " (*op. cit.*, p. 1). But there is (independent) reason to think the work to be pseudepigraphic.

The materials upon which his work relied were all drawn from the writings of others, however characteristic the stamp he put upon them. Al-Kindī was a *polymath* in the best sense of this term, a man of enormously diversified interest and wide-ranging erudition, based, in the final analysis, upon documentary sources.

What can be said regarding the nature of the " characteristic impress " which al-Kindī put upon the borrowed materials from which the fabric of his own were woven ? The key point here is his heavy reliance upon mathematics, which for al-Kindī was the first of the philosophical sciences, a position which virtually all later Arabic philosophers accorded to logic. A typical instance was encountered in the " Epistle on the Finitude of the Universe."⁹ Arguing, like Aristotle in Book I of *De Caelo*, against the impossibility of an infinite body, al-Kindī shifted the ground of the reasoning into a different arena. Aristotle's argumentation relied primarily upon physical consideration (primarily relating to weight and motion), while al-Kindī's is premissed entirely on mathematical considerations. This is typical of al-Kindī's mathematicizing tendency; we noted the same sort of geometrizing elaboration in the treatise in the concentric structure of the cosmos. In that opuscule, indeed, it appears clearly that al-Kindī is concerned not simply to expound certain facts about the universe, but to do this in such a way as to provide a striking and *explicit* illustration of the usefulness of mathematics as an instrument of scientific understanding.

This mathematicizing motive in al-Kindī was ably remarked a good many years ago by T. J. de Boer:

> Kindī's actual philosophy, like that of his contemporaries, consists, first and especially, of Mathematics and Natural Philosophy, in which Neo-Platonism and Neo-Pythagoreanism merge into one another. According to him no one can be a philosopher without studying Mathematics. Fanciful play upon letters and numbers is frequently met with in his writings. Mathematics he also applied to Medicine in his theory of the compound remedies. In fact he based the efficacy of these remedies, like the effect of music, upon geometrical proportion.¹⁰

De Boer's account of the matter is vividly substantiated in the

⁹ Tr. N. Rescher and H. Khatchadourian, " Al-Kindī's Epistle on the Finitude of the Universe," *Isis*, vol. 57 (1966), pp. 426–433.
¹⁰ *The History of Philosophy in Islam* (tr. by E. R. Jones; London, 1903), p. 100.

treatise on the Platonic solids, presented below, in which al-Kindī further indulges his predilection for what de Boer characterizes as " mathematical play."

Al-Kindī's style of discussion is distinctly *technical* in flavor. His mode of treatment exhibits a distinct predilection for technique: he is concerned not only to *develop* items of logico-mathematical machinery but to *apply* them. A noteworthy instance of this occurs in the treatise " On the quantity of the books of Aristotle and what is needful of them for the attainment of philosophy." [11] Throughout the treatise—even in its very title (*kamiyyah* = " quantity ")— al-Kindī strives to press the technical terminology of logic into the services of his presentation. He has the true technician's fondness for the tools of his trade.

The rationale for his favored mathematical approach is set out in a striking way in the " Epistle of the Finitude of the Universe ":

> So let us put an end to the maladies of verbal expressions so that there will be a [clear] pathway to what I wish to clarify for you, namely that it is impossible that the universe be unlimited—as many people think who have not advanced in the discipline of mathematics and do not understand logical reasoning . . .[12]

The use of a mathematical mode of exposition is clearly a cardinal point of doctrine with al-Kindī, a fact which accounts for his tendency to push recourse to supporting argumentation in the geometric mode substantially beyond the extent to which this was done in the Greek sources themselves. His penchant for mathematical reasoning is the basis of al-Kindī's sympathy for numerological considerations of a near-astrological kind. This kinship is sharply manifested in the treatise on the Platonic solids, where a great deal is made of such matters as the " masculine " and " feminine " nature of certain numbers. It must surely nowadays strike us as ironic that al-Kindī's very love of mathematical rigor in science inclined him toward the absurdities of neo-Pythagorean number-mysticism. We

---

[11] For the *editio princeps* of the Arabic text, together with an Italian translation, see M. Guidi and R. Walzer, " Studi su al-Kindī: I," *Atti della Reale Accademia dei Lincei*; Memorie della classe di scienze morali, etc.; series 6, vol. 6, fasc. 5 (Rome, 1940), pp. 375–390. Cf. N. Rescher, " Al-Kindī's Sketch of Aristotle's Organon " in *idem, Studies in the History of Arabic Logic* (Pittsburgh, 1963), pp. 28–38.
[12] *Op. cit.,* 187 : 3–6.

could, perhaps, afford to be even more patronizing about this if our own times had not some pretty bizarre efforts to force psychology and the social sciences to drink, *volens nolens*, from the springs of mathematical rigor.

In his important book on *La place d'Al-Fārābī dans l'école philosophique musulmane* (Paris, 1934), Ibrahim Madkour takes the view that al-Kindī can accurately be regarded as primarily a mathematician. Though there is much to be said on behalf of this view, as we have seen, it cannot, in the final analysis be accepted. For al-Kindī's resort to mathematics is not undertaken in its own right. With him, mathematics served, first and foremost, as an *instrument of demonstration*. The authentic mathematician cultivates his subject for its own sake; but for al-Kindī it is a working tool to be wielded for the pursuit of other disciplines.

Here, I think, we come to the heart both of al-Kindī's concept of scientific method and of the nature of his own " contribution." Science, on his view, is to be conceived of along Aristotelian lines, as at basis a matter of demonstration. But the pre-eminent instrument of demonstration is not logic, as with Aristotle, but mathematics. The neo-Pythagorean impress is heavily superimposed upon the neo-Platonic and the neo-Aristotelian materials. The paradigm science is of the type of astronomy or optics, where we can proceed *more geometrico*, by mathematical reasoning from evident premisses.

Given this approach to the matter, the character of al-Kindī's own contribution is readily appreciated. His originality in science does not lie in the devising of new materials, theories, or data. Rather, the genius of his work was the rigor with which he presented his ideas from the organizing perspective of the mathematical approach. The Platonic motto " Let no one ignorant of geometry enter here " should be inscribed in prominent letters on the keystone of the archway entrance to al-Kindī's philosophy.

Today we should be especially keen in our appreciation of al-Kindī's conception of method. Recent years have seen a fervent drive to devise mathematical structures in the human sciences, in emulation of the signal success of the physical sciences. Our appreciation for the mathematico-demonstrative methods should make us particularly sympathetic to al-Kindī's no doubt more

B

primitive but certainly no less enthusiastic tendency in the same direction.

3. Al-Kindī's Epistle

Our concern here is with a short physical treatise of al-Kindī's, his " Epistle (Showing) that the (Four) Elements and the Outermost Body are Spherical in Form " (*Risālah . . . fī anna al-ʿanaṣir wa-'l-jirm al-aqṣā kuriyyat al-shakl*). This treatise, whose existence was long known from Arabic biobibliographical sources, was rediscovered in 1931 by the eminent German orientalist Hellmuth Ritter in an Arabic manuscript codex (No. 4832) in the library of the Aya Sofya in Istanbul.[13] This material was examined around 1948 by the Egyptian scholar Dr. Muḥammad abū Rīdah, and was published by him in 1953 in the second volume of his collection of treatises by al-Kindī.[14] The English version of the epistle given below is its first rendition into a European language.

The objective of al-Kindī's short epistolary treatise is to establish that the structure of the cosmos is that of a nested series of concentric spheres : the exterior being the " outermost body " (i.e., the " sphere of the fixed stars "), and the spheres of the elements of earth and water (and air and fire ?) being placed concentrically, in that successive order, on the interior. It is remarkable that not a word is said about the " spheres " of air and fire. Either a part of the epistle is missing, or—and this seems more likely—the author expects the reader to adapt by himself the line of reasoning given about earth and water to the case of air and fire.

There are no ideas at work in al-Kindī's discussion that are not to be found in the corresponding passages of Ptolemy's *Almagest* [15] or

[13] A description of this material was published by Ritter and Martin Plessner, " Schriften Jaʿqūb ibn Isḥāq al-Kindī's in Stambuler Bibliotheken," *Archiv Orientálni*, vol. 4 (Prague, 1932), pp. 363–372.

[14] Muḥammad ʿAbd al-Hādī abū Rīdah (ed.), *Rasāʿil al-Kindī al-falsafiyyah*, 2 vols. (Cairo, 1950, 1953).

[15] Chs. 3–7 of Bk. I of Ptolemy's *Almagest* maintain the sphericity of the universe and of the earth, and argue that the earth is fixed in the center of the heavens (the loci of water, air, and fire are not discussed). Ptolemy's argument on these matters is not geometric, but descriptive.

indeed already in Aristotle's *Physics*.[16] Noteworthy, however, is the elaborate geometric machinery used by al-Kindī for presenting the argument. Both Aristotle and Ptolemy state the corresponding reasonings more descriptively and less geometrically than al-Kindī does. He seems to have an ulterior motive for this procedure: from the closing remarks it would appear that he wishes the epistle to serve as an inducement to the study of geometry by presenting a simple instance of the usefulness of this discipline as an instrument for scientific understanding of the world.

B. Translation of Al-Kindī's Epistle to Aḥmad ibn Al-Muʿtaṣim: "That the Elements and the Outermost Body Are Spherical in Form"[17]

Introduction—48: 9 [18]

(I shall present)[19] that whose clarification you asked for, in a brief way, (namely) that the bodies of the elements and the outermost body are spherical in form by the account of physics. (I do so) that it may serve as a reminder of what we said about this on special occasions, and save you the trouble of looking into a great deal of discourse (on the subject). I have sketched of this (topic) as much as I thought congenial to the power of your virtuous self and the skill of your perfect understanding. May God grant (me) success.

The Outermost Body—48: 14

Let us now say this: If it has been established that movement takes place about the center of the outermost body (i.e., that the outermost

---

[16] In ch. 4 of Bk. II of *De caelo*, Aristotle gives an argument to show that "the first heaven" is spherical, including (at 287a 31–287b 14) a geometric argument to show that water surrounds the earth spherically. And ch. 14 of Bk. II of the same treatise argues in a manner very close to that of al-Kindī (but descriptively rather than geometrically) that the earth is a sphere concentric with the heavenly sphere. For a detailed discussion of Aristotle's views and analyses of his arguments (including the mathematical argument of *De caelo*, II, iv) see Pierre Duhem, *Le Système du Monde*, vol. I (Paris, 1913; 1954 reprinting), pp. 211–219.

[17] Translated in collaboration with Professor Haig Khatchadourian.

[18] By these titles we indicate the starting point of each section in relation to abū Rīdah's text. The number on the left-hand side of the colon is the page number; the number on the right, the line number.

[19] The laudatory preliminaries addressed to the recipient of the epistle are omitted.

9

body revolves round its center), (and) that an unlimited body is an impossibility, then the limits (i.e., extremities) of the outermost body which moves around the center are (either) equidistant from its center, or are not. But if they are, the universe is necessarily spherical.

(On the other hand) if the extremities (limits) of the outermost body are not equidistant from the center of the universe, it would be possible for there to be in it (i.e., the universe) a finite sphere whose extremities (limits) are equidistant from the center of the universe. So if it has been established that no void or plenum—body or vacuum—lies outside the universe, it is impossible for the outermost body, having sides and angles, to revolve around the center of the universe, since a nonspherical body necessarily has sides and angles.

A demonstration of this will show that it is impossible. For if it were possible, then let the outermost body have sides and angles, as

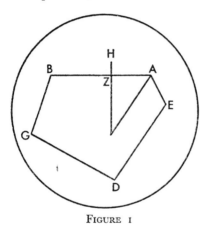

FIGURE 1

in figure *ABGDE* (Fig. 1). Let *W* be the center of the whole world, and let us join *W* with angle *A* and extend from *W* a line perpendicular to base *AB*, equal in length to *WA*. It cuts line *AB* in a right angle. We mark the point at which it intersects line *AB* by *Z*. Thus *AZW* is a right angle; and *AW* is the hypotenuse of *AZW*; and *AW* is longer than *WZ*. Further, let body *ABGDE* move (i.e., rotate), if that is possible, about *W*, which is the center of the universe—there being no void outside *ABGDE*, and no bodies—until point *A* reaches the place of point *H*. But there was neither a void nor a plenum in the interval between *Z* and *H*. So we write point *A* onto that line (i.e., line *WH*, now that *A* has reached *H*). It was therefore empty and a body was removed from it, moving beyond point *H* (as *WA* rotated to *WH*). The interval between *Z* and *H* is thus either a void or a plenum; and it was supposed that outside *Z* there was no void and no plenum. This contradiction is impossible. Therefore it is impossible for body *ABGDE* to revolve about the center of the universe which is W, if it has sides and angles. Hence the extremities (limits) of the outermost body, if the latter revolves round the center of the universe, have a spherical surface.

Earth and Water—50: 5

(As regards) those things (i.e., elements) that by their nature move toward the center—I mean earth and water—if some precede toward the center and others follow, then in accordance with their natures they (all) make their way toward the center and come to rest in as close proximity to the center as is possible for them. Thus no part of them (i.e., these elements), which is not separated from the center by earth or water, comes to rest until it reaches either the center or that which has preceded it to the center. Thus these two (elemental) bodies surround the center as surrounding spheres. Then if there is no interval (between them), then what is between them and the outermost sphere is spherical, since whatever lies between two concentric spheres must necessarily be spherical. For the moving body, as we have said, has a spherical extremity; and likewise a spherical interior. For if any angular body moved inside it, it would mingle and mix (with it) if it is a liquid capable of mixing. And if it is nonliquid—I mean something cohesive in nature—the outermost body will either come to rest and not move, (which is clearly not the case) or only those parts of it will move which did not lie between the angles of the body that is within it; and that (part of the outermost body) which moves with a circular motion will have a spherical interior (will be spherical on the inside), and the distance of the (outer) sphere's (inner) surface from the center of the universe will (then) be the distance of the angular surfaces from the center of the universe.

Thus the body of the universe is necessarily spherical, and that is what we wished to show.

Earth—50: 18

We say that that whose nature is to move toward the center of the universe cannot fail (either) to be created in the place which is peculiar to it, or to be created distributed in the universe. In this (second) case it, with all its parts, went to the center: it moved from the (other regions of) the universe toward the center, and those of its parts that arrived first came to rest at the center or as near to the center (as they could reach) on every side, and similarly with what followed them, until they were all at the center and that which is adjacent to it. In this way its different (extreme) parts come to be distant from the center by one and the same distance. It may however be that all its parts have been created in one place, or at a number of places outside the center. If they are at a number of places (outside the center), they would approach the center from all directions. So if they pressed toward the center with their forces in going there, they squeezed one another and met and came to be in places between which there was (before) a body of air, and so came to surround the center. Then if there remained any part of them whose distance from the center was greater than the distance of some other part, and it had some way (to get) closer to the center than by going in a straight line toward that part of the earth (that lay) beneath it, it would separate and go closer to the center by the easiest way. Similarly if it started from one place in the world outside the center.

An example of this is had when we suppose that the outermost body is circle *ABG* (Fig. 2), and point *D* the center of the universe.

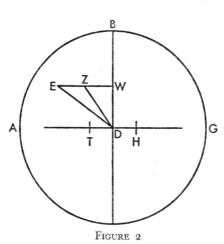

FIGURE 2

And the body going toward the center is body *EZW*. Then, I say that every part of body *EZW* goes toward the center from its own place, and (thus) it (i.e., some part) goes along line *ZD*: [20] *Z* goes along line *ZD*, and *W* [21] along line *WD*, and so it (i.e., part *ZW*) converges on surrounds) point *D*; and all the parts of *ZE* likewise go toward point *D* and converge on (surround) it. Anything else is impossible. For if it

[20] The text is corrupted; it reads *it goes along line EZD*.
[21] The text is corrupted; it reads *AW* for *W*.

were possible, and the body went as a whole, such that Z moved to D, then, since it (i.e., the body) is connected as a solid, if Z reached point D, W will reach point H and E point T. Hence not a single part of body EWZ except for Z reaches point D, which is the center, because if Z stopped at D the other parts (of EZW) would stop at places removed (from it) (i.e., D). This despite what we had assumed, (namely) that all the parts of body EZW went to D. But this consequence is impossible. Hence body EZW does not go to D as a connected unit, but rather with its parts separated. Each part goes to D (separately) and comes to rest at D or around D, depending on how fast or slowly it moved.

Thus the earth will necessarily be spherical and (located) at the center of the universe and this was what we wished to show.

Water—52: 10

That being so, let us (next) show that the surface of the water is likewise spherical, even if it is (initially) (placed) over a portion of the earth, which is not spherical.

This would be the case if we supposed that the portion of the earth which is not spherical (and on which the water is initially placed) is

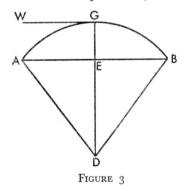

FIGURE 3

line GW (Fig. 3), and point D is the center of the universe; and the point at which line AB is bisected is E. Let us extend a line from it (i.e., E) to D. Arc AGB (lies about) the center of the earth. Let us join arc AGB and W (i.e., join G and W). And let $ABGD$ be on one plane. Let us (also) continue line DE to point G. Then lines AD,[22] BD, DG are equal, since they radiate from center D to circumference AGB; and DE is a part of GD; and GD is equal to each of the two lines AD and DB; and ED is a perpendicular line. Water naturally moves to the center. But if obstructed from

[22] Editor's note: " In the original, AB, which does not fit the meaning of the passage."

(reaching) the center—I mean the center of the universe—it will (move) to the places closest to the center of the universe. Hence water, if it flows from point A on surface AB, will flow to point E; because it (point E) is nearer to D than A is, and than B is. Likewise if (the water) flowed from B it will stop at it (point E). Similarly if (it) always flowed in the direction of E till it reached point G, its distance from D will become (the same) as the distance of A from D, and B from D. Hence if it reached the places that are equally distant as G (from the center), it will not flow in any (more distant) direction, (and) will not stop at a surface exterior to arc AGB—anything else is impossible. For if it (i.e., the water) flowed to some other place which is further from D, which is the center of the universe [23]—if it flowed (to W) from G or A or B—it flows to a place farther from D than that from which it flowed. Hence, by its natural motion, it moved away from the center of the universe. It has already been said that water naturally flows toward the center of the universe, and that was assumed. Thus this consequence is impossible. Hence it is not possible that the surface of the water be nonspherical; which was what we wished to show.

Conclusion—53: 13

It has thus been shown from the perspective of physics that the surface of the water is spherical, and also that all the elements and the remotest body are spherical.

It is possible for us to show that the body of the universe is a sphere by the propaedeutic disciplines (viz. by mathematics). Let us now therefore perfect this art with the aid of the Almighty and with His strengthening.

The epistle is finished. Thanks be given to God, Lord of the worlds. May His blessings be upon His prophet Muḥammad and his whole people.

---

[23] Editor's note: " The entire passage is confused, and perhaps is incomplete; this has prevented us from attempting to emend it, but the general meaning is clear."

II

AL-KINDĪ'S TREATISE
ON THE PLATONIC SOLIDS

A. INTRODUCTION

1. General Observations Regarding the Nature of al-Kindī's Treatise

Like most of his short treatises, al-Kindī's tract *Fī 'l-sabab alladhi (lahu) nasabat al-quadamā' al-ashkāl al-khamsah ilā 'l-usṭuqussāt* ("On the reason why the ancients ascribed the five figures to the [four] elements ") addresses itself to a single specialized problem stated at the outset (54: 9–10): What reason led " the ancient philosophers " (not—be it noted—Plato specifically!) to attribute the five figures to the four elements. The basis of al-Kindī's treatise is clearly the discussion in the *Timaeus* (53c–56c) which assigns four of the five regular, " Platonic " solids to the four elements and the remaining one to " the whole." As we shall see in detail in Sect. 6 below, al-Kindī's discussion corresponds with Plato's in most significant points.

The first part of the treatise (roughly two-thirds its length) provides a straightforward answer to the question raised in its title. But then (at 60: 10) a transition occurs and a shift is made to the metaphysical or even theological theme " how nature has indicated . . . that the cause of everything is a single one without any plurality." The rest of the treatise deals briefly with three matters: (1) the preeminence of the sphere over the five regular solids, (2) the uniqueness of the immaterial, and (3) cosmic and divine unity. These topics have increasingly less relationship to the discussion of regular solids and elements of the first part of the treatise—although all of them do represent themes also touched upon in the *Timaeus*. This elaboration, however, serves to make good the claim which al-Kindī had put forward at the outset (54: 11–12) that the treatise deals with " some of the profitable achievements in the trade whose market is the cultivation of the unity of God." It is clear that al-Kindī is eager to show that philosophical and scientific conceptions not only do not conflict with religion, but even serve to confirm and support some of the key tenets of Islam.

2. *The Background and Sources of the Treatise*

Plato's *Timaeus* exercised a vast influence in late antiquity. Even the middle Stoa was much interested in it, as witness the commentary of Poseidonius of Apamei (b. ca. 135 B.C.).[1] The middle Platonists gave it a prominent place: There are commentaries or partial commentaries by Plutarch (fl. ca. 100 A.D.), Theon of Smyrna (fl. ca. 100), Gaius (fl. ca. 130), Albinus (fl. ca. 150) and others.[2] The later Peripatetics also studied the work, e.g., Adrastus of Aphrodisias (fl. ca. 120 A.D.).[3] The neo-Platonists of course placed the greatest weight upon it, the important commentary by Proclus assuring its influence. (The Latin translation (to 53b) and commentary of Chalcidius (fl. ca. 350) made the *Timaeus* the only Platonic text to be available in Latin until ca. 1150.)

What did al-Kindī know of Plato's dialogue? The answer to this question is straightforward and decisive: he had immediate access to the whole of this treatise in the Arabic translation (made around 820) of Yaḥyā (or Yuḥanna) ibn al-Biṭrīq (d. ca. 830).[4] Also, al-Kindī could, at the time of writing his treatise, very possibly have had access to Galen's Compendium of the *Timaeus*, put into Arabic (around 860) by Ḥunain ibn Isḥāq (d. 877) and/or his pupil

---

[1] K. Praechter, *Die Philosophie des Altertums* (= vol. I of *Friederich Ueberwegs Grundriss der Geschichte der Philosophie*, Berlin, 1926), p. 478. Cf. Sarton, IHS, vol. I, p. 204.

[2] See *ibid.*, pp. 533, 540, 541, 546–554. And cf. R. E. Witt, *Albinus and the History of Middle Platonism* (Cambridge, 1937).

[3] Sarton, IHS, vol. I, p. 271.

[4] For this scholar see Brockelmann, GAL, I, pp. 221–222 (old ed., p. 203); SI, p. 364; as well as D. M. Dunlop, " The Translations of al-Biṭrīq and Yaḥyā (Yuḥannā) b. al-Bitriq," *Journal of the Royal Asiatic Society*, 1959, pp. 140–150. His translation was later revised by Yaḥyā ibn ʿAdī (d. 974).

'Īsā ibn Yaḥyā ibn Ibrāhīm (d. ca. 910).[5] Moreover, he may well also have had partial access to Galen's Commentary on the *Timaeus*, extensive parts of which had been put into Arabic.[6]

Although a detailed account of the reception of the *Timaeus* in Arabic philosophy has yet to be written, we know that it aroused considerable interest in the century from 850 to 950. Al-Kindī, al-Rāzī (Rhazes), and al-Fārābī [7] all dealt with this work. Al-Rāzī even adopted its notoriously un-Islamic teaching—its teaching at any rate in the view of such interpreters as Plutarch and Galen—that creation of an orderly world, a *cosmos*, was not *ex nihilo*, but from preexisting, indeed eternal matter.[8] The earliest generation of Arabic philosophers apparently considered this work to be of greatest importance for the understanding of Greek philosophy, and it excited great interest upon its first entry into an Arabic milieu.

However, while the primary inspiration of al-Kindī's treatise is patently Platonic, it is clear that he saw Plato through Aristotelian eyes. One sign of this is the prominent use of the form-matter dichotomy (e.g., at 59: 13–60: 1). A second is its discussion (55: 18 ff.) of the concentric organization of the cosmos in accordance with the inwards or outwards tendency of the elements, which, in the details added to Plato's discussion at *Timaeus* 32b, follows faithfully the treatment of Aristotle's *De Caelo*. Another example is the discussion of the superiority of the sphere and its claims to primacy in the structure of the cosmos (60: 13–61: 14), which adds to Plato's discussion at *Tim.* 33d–34a some Aristotelian touches—e.g., al-Kindī relates this discussion to the Aristotelian thesis that " it is not possible that there be any actual thing that does not have limits " (61: 14). It is also interesting that al-Kindī speaks, with deliberate vagueness, of the

---

[5] Paul Kraus and Richard Walzer, *Galeni Compendium Timaei Platonis* (*Plato Arabus*, vol. I, London, 1951), pp. 18–21. On the theme of the present treatise Galen's compendium is, however, brief and superficial as compared with al-Kindī's elaborate treatment.

[6] See Moritz Steinschneider's discussion in Virchov's *Archiv*, vol. 124 (1891).

[7] " The Philosophy of Plato and Aristotle," tr. M. Mahdi (New York, 1962), pp. 45, 65–66.

[8] Walzer, *Greek into Arabic* (Oxford, 1962), p. 16. (Cf. al-Fārābī's discussion in *Alfārābī's Philosophische Abhandlungen*, tr. F. Dieterici (Leiden, 1892), pp. 35 ff.) The neo-Platonic tradition on which Rhazes relied viewed the *Timaeus* as Plato's most important work: Proclus, indeed, was ready to dispense with the rest.

fact that " ancient philosophers " attributed the five figures to the four elements (54: 9–10): there is no specific statement that Plato did, and no hint that Aristotle did not. In al-Kindī we have another instance of that Platonic-Aristotelian syncretism that was found in the earliest generation of Arabic philosophers, for example al-Fārābī.[9] Prominent too in al-Kindī's treatise are various Pythagorean numerological notions—some derived from but others added to Plato's *Timaeus*—which are also stressed in the thought of Rhazes.[10]

3. The Rationale of the Treatise

The four (mundane or sublunary) elements are earth, water, air, and fire, to which a fifth, celestial material (aether) may be added as constituent of the outer heavens. In al-Kindī's treatise, as in Plato's *Timaeus* and Aristotle's *De Caelo*, these are thought of as distributed in the universe in a concentric pattern:

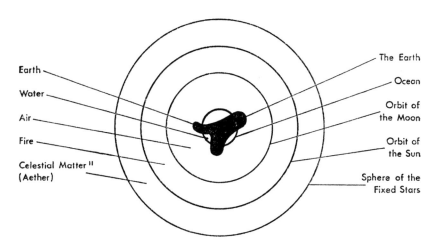

Earth

Water

Air

Fire

Celestial Matter [11]
(Aether)

The Earth

Ocean

Orbit of the Moon

Orbit of the Sun

Sphere of the Fixed Stars

[9] See his treatise on " The Harmony Between the Views of Plato and Aristotle " published by F. Dieterici, *Alfārābī's Philosophische Abhandlungen* (Leiden, 1890) translated into German by Dieterici under the same title (Leiden, 1892).

[10] Max Meyerhof, " The Philosophy of the Physician al-Rāzī," *Islamic Culture*, vol. 15 (1941), pp. 45–58.

[11] Some authorities have it that for Plato (unlike Aristotle) this region is also one of Fire, a view strongly supported by the discussion of the distribution of the four elements at *Timaeus* 32b–33b. On this basis the only possible role for a celestial material would be the composition of the sphere of the fixed stars itself.

The four mundane elements are thought to be associated with the so-called " four opposites," hot-cold and moist-dry, in such a way that each element embodies one member of each pair of opposites, as follows:

	Hot	Cold
Moist:	Air	Water
Dry:	Fire	Earth

The five Platonic solids are as follows:

Regular Solid	Type of Base	No. of Bases	No. of Edges
Tetrahedron	Triangle	4	6
Hexahedron (Cube)	Square	6	12
Octahedron	Triangle	8	12
Dodecahedron	Pentagon	12	30
Icosahedron	Triangle	20	30

Plato, and al-Kindī following him, established the following correlation between the regular solids and the elements:

Element	Regular Solid
Earth	Hexahedron (Cube)
Water	Icosahedron
Air	Octahedron
Fire	Tetrahedron
Celestial Material (Aether) [12]	Dodecahedron

This assignment of regular solids is based on various characteristics both of the *microstructure* of the elements—the various physical properties which they exhibit in the small, rather than on considerations having to do with their characteristics on a grander scale— and of the *macrostructure* of their distribution in the universe. This

[12] There is room for question whether Plato intended (i) to assign the dodecahedron specifically to the celestial material (*aether*) on rigid analogy with the assignment of the other regular solids to the four mundane elements, or (ii) to assign the dodecahedron symbolically to " the whole " generally, without any such physico-structural implications. The second view finds support in the fact that the fifth type of matter (*aether*) does not explicitly figure in the *Timaeus* at all, but first appears explicitly in the *Epinomis* (981c). On the other hand, Plutarch and various other ancient authorities support the first alternative. (The data are set out in Cornford's commentary, on pp. 220–221.) Al-Kindī's treatment is indecisive and leaves the issue as vague as does the *Timaeus* itself, although it seems likely (in view of the discussion at 6o: 13 ff.) that he would assign to " the whole " not a regular solid, but the sphere.

latter consideration is interestingly akin to Kepler's use of the regular solids to account for the respective distances between the planets in terms of a series of regular solids inscribed within the bounding orbital spheres of one another: [13]

Mercury
  }Octahedron
Venus
  }Icosahedron
The Earth
  }Dodecahedron
Mars
  }Tetrahedron
Jupiter
  }Hexahedron (Cube)
Saturn

Specifically, some of the characteristic grounds upon which al-Kindī bases the assignment of solids to elements are as follows:

(1) *Numerological Ratios.* A typical mode of argument is as follows: " Because twelve is to six in a whole ratio, and the whole is greater than the component distances, and because this ratio is that of the first simplest multiple (viz. 2), therefore the one (solid) with twelve (bases) was attributed to that (which lies at) the (remotest) extremity from the earth: I mean the sky which is of one (type) with the earth, since both are extremities of the universe " (56: 5-7). Or again: " As to the solid with twenty bases, the ratio of its bases to the bases of the (solid) with four bases is in a ratio of multiples of five (viz. 20 : 4 :: 5 : 1). . . . Similarly its thirty sides are to the six sides of the (solid) with four bases in the ratio of multiples of five also (i.e., 30 : 6 :: 5 : 1). Thus the (solid) with twenty bases was ascribed to the element opposite to fire [already correlated with the tetrahedron] in both of its qualities (viz. hot and dry) together. (That is, to water, which is cold and wet.) " (58: 14-17.)

(2) *Masculine-Feminine.* Even numbers are " feminine," admitting of division into two equal parts, and odd numbers are " masculine,"

---

[13] It is common knowledge that the same neo-Pythagorean and neo-Platonic influences to which al-Kindī was subject weighed heavily with Kepler.

admitting of no such division. Only one solid (the hexahedron) has bases (viz. cubes) with an even number of edges (unlike triangles and pentagons). " Since the feminine is inferior to the masculine, and the earth is below all, this form is ascribed to the earth " (55: 19–20).

(3) *Activity-Passivity.* We prominently find such reasonings as: " The (solid) with eight bases was ascribed to the element (viz. air) which shares with fire in the stronger quality of activity " (58: 12).

(4) *Movable versus Stable Numbers (Tendencies to " Increase " or " Decrease ").* A number is " stable " if, like 6, it equals the sum of its divisors. When a number is not stable, it is " movable ": if its divisors sum to less than it (e.g., 8) it tends to a decrease or " more to the lesser," and if its divisors sum to more than it (e.g., 12) it tends to increase or " more to the greater." We find such reasonings as: " The solid with eight bases—because of the slowness of its motion to the lesser—(was ascribed) to air which is slower in motion (than fire) " (59: 2–3).

(5) *Physical Characteristics of the Solids (Fineness/Denseness, Lightness, Heaviness).* Under this heading the following reasoning is typical: " The finest of them (the solids) since it has the fewest bases . . . and since it is the sharpest because it has the sharpest angles was attributed to fire, since it (viz. fire) is the sharpest of the three (remaining) elements and the finest of them " (57: 6–8). Or again: " The (solid) with twelve pentagonal bases [was attributed to the sky because it] equals in its number of bases the twelve constellations which are prescribed for the celestial sphere " (56: 19–20).

(6) *The Six Elemental " Factors."* Considerable use is made of the pertinence to the various elements of certain " factors," viz.:

(i) matter

(ii) form

(iii) that by which there is motion with respect to place without opposition

(iv) generation (of plant and animal life)

(v) stability of state

(vi) intelligent action

21

These are exhibited by the elements as follows:

Earth: (i)–(iii), (iv)
Water: (i)–(iii)
Air: (i)–(iii)
Fire: (i)–(iii)
The Celestial Sphere: (i)–(iii), (v), (vi)

This is taken to account for the attribution to earth of the hexahedron (cube) with its four-sided bases, to celestial matter of the dodecahedron with its pentagonal bases, and to the other elements of the regular solids with triangular bases.

*   *   *

It is clear, then, that the rationale of al-Kindī's arguments to support the correlation of elements with the regular solids takes into account on the one hand the physical characteristics of the elements and the geometric characteristics of the solids and then establishes a linkage between them on the basis of numerological ones found in or imputed to these characteristics.

4. The Correlation Between al-Kindī's Treatise and Plato's Timaeus

There is a patent and substantial kinship between al-Kindī's treatise and corresponding parts of the *Timaeus*. This relationship is exhibited by the following tabulation:

Topic	Kindi	Timaeus
Description of the Figures and their Argument to the Elements	54: 4–60: 9	55d–56b
Superiority of the Sphere over the Regular Solids	60: 13–61: 14	33b
Uniqueness of the Immaterial	61: 15–62: 10	30c–31a
Cosmic and Divine Unity	61: 11–62: 5	31a–31b; 55c–55d

A few examples of specific parallels are:

K.	T.
The spherical figure is contained within one single surface without any plurality, and does not depart from its own nature. . . . By the existence of the sphere there exists each one of the rest (of the figures). (60: 13–60: 16)	The [most] fitting shape would be a figure that comprehends in itself all the figures there are [viz. the sphere] . . . a figure the most perfect and uniform of all. (33b)
The one (regular solid) with six bases (i.e., the cube) was attributed to the earth, which is the stable element in comparison with the rest of the elements, being located beneath them all. (56: 2–56: 3)	To earth let us assign the cubical figure, for of all the four kinds (i.e., elements) earth is the most immobile. . . . (55e)
The finest of them [i.e., of the regular solids], since it has the fewest bases—that is four triangular bases—and since it is the sharpest because it has the sharpest angles, was attributed to fire, since it is the sharpest of the three (remaining) elements and the finest of them. (57: 6–57: 8)	Now, taking all the figures, the one with the fewest faces (i.e., tetrahedron or pyramid) must be the most mobile, since it has the sharpest cutting edges and the sharpest points in every direction, and moreover the lightest, as being composed of the smallest number of similar parts. . . . Hence . . . among the solid figures we have constructed, we may take the pyramid as the element or seed of fire. (56a–b)

Numerous other parallels between al-Kindī's discussion and Plato's can be found—some of them being indicated in the footnotes to our translation of al-Kindī's treatise.

Just as striking, however, as the points of agreement between al-Kindī's treatment and the *Timaeus* are the points of difference. Thus Plato's discussion has relevant features upon which al-Kindī does not touch. Instances are the construction of solids out of triangles (54b–55c), and the elaborate discussion of the transformation of the elements into one another (56c–57c). These differences appear to arise from the fact that Plato's correlation of the regular solids with the elements is carried through primarily at the small scale (*micro*) level (*Timaeus*, 56b–56c) with respect to the constitution of the elements, whereas al-Kindī treats them almost exclusively on the cosmic (*macro*) level.

C

STUDIES IN ARABIC PHILOSOPHY

On the other hand, al-Kindī's discussion goes far beyond the *Timaeus* in giving grounds for the correlation between the elements and the regular solids. His discussion takes account of considerations not even hinted at in the *Timaeus*—primarily with respect to numerological detail. It is clear that al-Kindī had learned to see the matters dealt with in the *Timaeus* from the angle of neo-Pythagorean considerations, and that the discussions which introduced these matters to him were heavily laden with neo-Platonic elaborations of the materials of Plato's dialogue.

5. Technical Matters Regarding the Text and the Translation

The Arabic text of al-Kindī's treatise survives in a unique Istanbul manuscript in the codex (Aya Sofya 4832) discussed in Sect. 3 of the preceding chapter. A transcription of this manuscript text was published in 1953 by Muḥammad abū Rīdah in the second volume of his edition of the *Rasā'il al-Kindī al-falsafiyyah* (two vol's, Cairo, Dār al-fikr al-'arabī, 1950, 1953).

The translation given in Part B strives to be reasonably literal. The division into sections and into paragraphs, however, is in most instances without manuscript warrant and dictated by the sense of the discussion alone. Even the division into sentences is, as any Arabist knows, to some extent arbitrary.

The bracketed numbering in the translation establishes its correlation with Abū Rīdah's Arabic text, with the indicated transitions from line to line. For obvious grammatical reasons such a division cannot but be occasionally imperfect.

B. Al-Kindī's Treatise
"On the Reason Why the Ancients Attributed the Five Figures to the Elements"

(Preface)

[54: 6] May God protect you, my praiseworthy brother, from every perplexity! And may He make easy for you the path of deliverance from the pitfalls /7/ of harmful doubt and the darkness of shameful ignorance! May He grant you knowledge which would lead you to deeds that bring you closer to Him! /8/ May He thus make you happy to the end of your life!

/9/ I understood that you asked to be informed of the reason which led the ancient philosophers to ascribe /10/ the five figures to the four elements and to the celestial sphere, and how this ascription (was made).

/11/ I am thus obliged to consider undertaking to inform you about this, it being one of the profitable works in the trade of one whose market /12/ is to establish the oneness of God, the All-high and the All-mighty, (to demonstrate) that to Him belongs the power that creates all things, /13/ that He possesses everything, (and) that His is the most perfect action. It is the practice of the best people of every trade not to neglect anything profitable for their trade from /14/ wherever it springs forth and grows.[14]

/15/ Therefore I hasten (to respond) to your wish about this, with a view to its lasting profits and its flourishing fruits in proportion to [55: 1] what my intellect attained of them and what I perceived of their hidden indications secretly concealed within the folds of their profound and deep statements. /2/ I did not stint any good counsel or efforts in explaining this by the simplest (possible) discussion. May the Giver of good things grant us success in everything /3/ praiseworthy (in) religion.

(The Attribution of Regular Solids to the Elements)

/4/ As regards the matter in hand [15] I think that the reasons why each one of the five (regular) bodies that fall within the sphere /5/ —each one of which has bases with equal sides, namely (i) that with four triangular bases /6/ attributed to fire, (ii) that with six square bases attributed to earth, (iii) that with /7/ eight triangular bases attributed to air, (iv) that with twelve pentagonal bases attributed to the celestial sphere, and (v) that with /8/ twenty triangular bases attributed to water—were attributed to the four elements and the celestial sphere are as I shall (now) describe:

---

[14] The economic analogy is provocative. The formulation re-echoes Koranic passages where good acts are likened to profitable and bad acts to unprofitable commerce. (See *Qur'ān*, II: 15; LXI: 10.)

[15] Literally: *As regards (that which comes) after this.*

/9/ Firstly this was because they (i.e., the regular solids) are just five, neither more nor less, the same number as that of the four elements composed-of-opposites /10/ and the fifth nature which is removed from the opposites. Three of them are bounded by triangles, one by squares, /11/ and one by pentagons. One of them has four triangles and six edges; one has eight triangles /12/ and twelve edges; one has twenty triangular faces and thirty edges; one has six /13/ squares and twelve edges; and one has twelve pentagons and thirty edges also. The number /14/ of the surfaces of each of them is also even. As to the figures of the bases, each of them is odd except only one /15/ which is even: I mean that all of them are pentagons and triangles which are odd, but one of them is a square, /16/ which is even. The odd numbers are related to the masculine, because it is not divisible and does not admit /17/ of passivity. And the even numbers are related to the feminine, because it is divisible and admits of passivity.

(*The Hexahedron—Earth*)

/18/ Since the one (regular solid) having six square bases is the only even one of them, it is completely related to the feminine and contradicts /19/ all the rest of them. Since the feminine is inferior to the masculine, and the earth is below all, this form is ascribed /20/ to the earth. Also since it has six bases, and six is a stable, firm number without any tendency to increase /21/ or decrease.[16] The rest (of the regular solids)—I mean the one with four, and that with eight, and that with twelve, and that with twenty (bases)—[56: 1] some have a decreasing number and some an increasing one (i.e., number), and all tend from completeness to an increase or a decrease, and are not stable /2/ in respect of their numbers. (Therefore) the one with six bases was attributed to the earth, which is the stable element in comparison with the rest of the elements, /3/ being located beneath them all, so that everything tends towards it. And because the six (faced solid) encloses its parts, and the rest do not /4/ block in their parts, the six (faced solid) was ascribed to the blocked-in earth and the rest to the free-flowing (elements).

---

[16] This (as will appear below) comes from the fact that 6 equals the sum of its divisors 1, 2, and 3.

(*Dodecahedron—Celestial Sphere*)

/5/ Because twelve is to six in a whole ratio (or: *relation*), and the whole is greater than the component distances, /6/ and because this ratio is that of the first simplest multiple (viz. 2), therefore the one (solid) with twelve [17] (bases) was attributed to /7/ that (which lies at) the (remotest) extremity from the earth: I mean the sky which is of one (type) with the earth, since both are extremities (i.e., the one inner and the other outer) of the universe. The extremities /8/ which are (extremities) of the universe are the most extreme of extremities: they are the most distant of the component distances in respect of place. (Thus) they are both (viz. earth and sky) united in their power and their nature.

/9/ Because all things that are confined are bounded by odd bases—and the (regular solid) with twelve bases is alone /10/ in being enclosed by pentagons—therefore the three figures enclosed by triangles, since they are enclosed by a single (uniform) figure, /11/ were attributed to the three elements which are in a single (uniform) motion, i.e., rectilinear motion, namely fire /12/ and air, and water. The one (regular solid) with twelve bases, which is enclosed by pentagons which differ from triangles was (thus) attributed to the sky /13/ which differs in its movement from the three enclosed elements.

/14/ Further, (this was done) because it is not fitting for the (celestial) sphere (to be associated with) the figure of a (solid) with equal sides and equal angles, which (i.e., whose surface) is divided /15/ into triangles which are the corners of every (remaining) figure that possesses (equal) sides, each single side being a base for an equilateral and equiangular triangle, /16/ except the pentagon. For it is divisible into five equilateral and equiangular triangles, /17/ just as is the case with the (solid) with twenty bases, (for) every five of its (equilateral) triangles (make up) an equilateral and equiangular pentagon— /18/ (and therefore) the (solid) with twelve bases was attributed to the body that moves with a spherical motion. (This was done) also /19/ because the (solid) with twelve pentagonal bases equals in its number of bases the twelve constellations which

---

[17] The text mistakenly reads: *twenty*.

27

are prescribed /20/ for the celestial sphere.[18] Each one of its (pentagonal) bases is divisible into five triangles equal in number to the five boundaries prescribed for every /21/ constellation. The sides (edges) of the (solid) with twelve bases are thirty, equal to the divisions of that part of [57: 1] the twelve (sections) prescribed for the celestial sphere, which is called a degree.[19] The number of triangles into which the pentagons are divided /2/ is sixty, equivalent to the sextant (i.e., 60°). The sides of these sixty triangles (amount to) ninety, equivalent to the quadrants.[20] /3/ These two figures, I mean the sextant and the quadrant, are the supports of the figures that are the supporting-pedestals of the rest of the prescribed celestial sphere.[21] /4/ Because the " triple " (30°) is weaker than the sextant (60°) and (it is) also weaker than the quadrant (90°), it was agreed to ascribe /5/ the (solid) with twelve bases to the body of the celestial sphere.

(Tetrahedron, Octahedron, Dodecahedron—Fire, Air, Water)

/6/ As to the three odd (regular solids) attributed to the remaining three elements, the finest of them, since it has the fewest /7/ bases— that is, four triangular bases—and since it is the sharpest because it has the sharpest angles, was attributed to /8/ fire, since it (viz. fire) is the sharpest of the three (remaining) elements and the finest of them. The (solid) with eight bases—which follows in the number /9/ of bases and the sharpness of angles—was attributed to air, which follows fire in fineness and sharpness. The (solid) with twenty /10/ bases—since it follows the one with eight bases in the number of bases and the sharpness of angles—was attributed to water which follows /11/ air in fineness and sharpness.

/12/ Furthermore, since the (solid) with twenty bases is the most distant of these three odd (regular solids) from /13/ the one with four bases, these two figures from among these three odd (solids) (viz. the tetrahedron and the icosahedron) were attributed to the two opposite elements (viz. fire and water), /14/ because

---

[18] Cf. *Timaeus*, 55c, and Cornford's comment thereupon.
[19] That is, the 360° circle can be divided into 12 sections of 30° each.
[20] Each quadrant has 90 degrees.
[21] One cannot but wonder what sort of model was at issue here.

opposites are the most distantly removed limits. And because the more composite is the denser and the heavier, /15/ the (solid) composed of more bases (viz. the icosahedron) was attributed to the denser and heavier of the two elements, viz. water, and the one composed of fewer bases (viz. the tetrahedron) /16/ (was attributed) to the finer and lighter, viz. fire.

As for the (odd regular solid) intermediate between the (ones with) the most and the fewest bases (viz. the octahedron), /17/ it was attributed to the (element) intermediate between the two opposite elements in fineness and density and in lightness and heaviness, viz. air.

(Activity and Passivity)

/18/ They have done so because the masculine contains the active qualities possessed by heat and the passive qualities [58: 1] by dryness, and the active is stronger than the passive. Fire possesses heat and dryness, therefore air shares with it (i.e., fire) /2/ in the heat which is their active quality. The active is stronger than and superior to the passive, because the passive stands /3/ to the active like prime matter (al-hiwlā = hylē), and the active is to it like form.[22] The earth shares (with fire) in the dryness which is their passive quality, /4/ and the passive is inferior and weaker than the active.

The twelve sides (i.e., edges) of the (solid) with eight bases are (related) to /5/ the six [23] sides of the (solid) with four bases also in the whole (entire) ratio (or: *relation*) (i.e., $12 \div 6 = 2$). And the twelve sides of the (solid) with six /6/ bases are (related) to the six sides of the (solid) with four bases in a whole (entire) ratio also (i.e., $12 \div 6 = 2$). /7/ But the relation of the six bases of the (solid) with six bases to the four bases of the (solid) with four bases /8/ are not in a whole (entire) ratio but in a partial (i.e., fractional) [24] ratio which is a ratio removed from /9/ the whole (entire) ratio. Therefore the (solid) with four bases was ascribed to fire, since it has (1) a relation (ratio) to the (solid) with eight bases in /10/ two ways among the strongest ratios of composition, and (2) a relation to the

---

[22] That is we have the proportion—active : passive :: form : matter.
[23] The text mistakenly reads: *four.*
[24] We suppose the doubtful word to be *bi-juz'.*

(solid) with six bases in one way also among the strongest /11/ ratios of composition and (3) a firm relation which is the intermediate one in power among the strongest ratios of composition. /12/ (Thus) the (solid) with eight bases was ascribed to the element (viz. air) which shares with fire in the stronger quality of activity. And /13/ the (solid) with six bases was ascribed to the element (viz. earth) which shares with fire in the weaker quality of passivity.

/14/ As to the (solid) with twenty bases, the ratio of its bases to the bases of the (solid) with four bases is in a ratio of multiples of five (viz. 20 : 4 :: 5 : 1). /15/ This ratio is not in any way in the ratio of composition. Similarly, its thirty sides are to /16/ the six sides of the (solid) with four bases in the ratio of multiples of five also (i.e., 30 : 6 :: 5 : 1). Thus the (solid) with twenty bases /17/ was ascribed to the element opposite to fire in both its qualities (viz. hot and dry) together. (That is, to water, which is cold and wet.)

(Movable Numbers)

/18/ Furthermore the (solid) with four bases and the (solid) with eight bases have " movable " numbers which are not complete /19/ and not stable, as was previously said regarding the number of the complete and stable ratio (relation).[25]   Both of them are " movable " to the lesser, /20/ because the parts of four are one-half (i.e., 2) and one-quarter (i.e., 1), and the total of three (i.e., 2 + 1) is less than four. Similarly, the parts of eight are /21/ lesser. (Since the divisors of 8, viz. 1, 2, 4, have the sum 7 < 8.) Thus both share together in the movement to the lesser. (Therefore) they were ascribed to the two elements /22/ which are liquid and movable, sharing [26] in a motion in one single (common) direction (viz. upwards from earth and water) I mean fire and air. [59: 1] And of these two, the (solid) with four bases was ascribed to fire, because its motion to the lesser is the strongest of the two, since its parts are more distant in relation /2/ to it than the parts of the (solid) with eight bases (are distant) from eight.[27]   And the (solid) with eight

---

[25] See 55: 20–56: 2 above.

[26] Delete the superfluous *sin* in the printed Arabic text.

[27] That is, the divisors of 4 are 1 and 2, whose sum is 3 < 4; the divisors of 8 are 1, 2, 4, whose sum is 7 < 8. But 3 is (proportionally) more remote from 4 than 7 is from 8.

bases—because of the slowness its motion /3/ to the lesser—(was ascribed) to air which is slower in motion. The (solid) with twenty bases whose motion is opposite to the motion /4/ of (both) the (solid) with four bases and the (solid) with eight bases—since the motion of the former [28] is to the lesser and the motion of the latter is to the greater, /5/ because the parts of the twenty are greater than twenty [29] by one-tenth of twenty (viz. by 2)—was ascribed to the third liquid element (i.e., to water), /6/ whose movement opposes the movement of fire and air, since both their motions are away from and its motion is towards the center.

/7/ As to the figure which is bounded by twelve bases, inasmuch as the number of its bases is in an increasing number by a third /8/ of it [30]—the proportion of its increase to it being the greatest (largest) proportion of the motion of increase or lessening (decrease). —Therefore the (solid) with twelve /9/ bases was ascribed to the celestial sphere, because its motion towards an increase is swifter than that of all the motions we have described—the motion /10/ of the celestial sphere being swifter than the motions of the (four mundane) elements—and furthermore because the sky is the place (locus) of the spirits which have intellects /11/ that are pure and unmixed intelligences, and are immortal by nature, unlike the rest of what God has created. The earth /12/ is the generator of everything grown or born, I mean that everything grown or born is based upon it and has its being through it.

(The Earth—Second Consideration in the Light of the " Five Factors ")

/13/ Thus every one of the (four terrestrial) elements and the sky is the possessor of (i) prime matter (*hylē*) and of (ii) form and of (iii) that by which there is uniform motion /14/ with respect to place. In the earth there is the special circumstances that it is the generator of everything grown or born. [31] In the sky there is stability /15/ of

[28] Reading *dhālika* for *dh-y-n-k*.

[29] That is, the divisors of 20, viz. 1, 2, 4, 5, 10, have sum 22 > 20.

[30] I.e., the divisors of 12 are 1, 2, 3, 4, and 6, whose sum is 16 = 12 + 4, 4 being one-third of twelve.

[31] For the doubtful words I read exactly as in line 12 above. Compare also line 19 below.

state and also intelligent action. (Thus) the earth has fourness in its composition, and the sky has fiveness /16/ in its composition. The primary figures (viz. the tetra-, octa-, and icosahedron) all have triangles as sides, because anything that has sides /17/ is (either) a triangle or is divisible into triangles, (while) a triangle is not decomposible into anything else (than triangles). Because primary (factors of) sensibles /18/ are, as we have mentioned, prime matter and form and that by which there is motion, (therefore) the earth, the owner of [32] /19/ four (factors)—I mean matter and form and that by which there is uniform motion with respect to place and generation—was ascribed to /20/ that (solid) which is enclosed by squares (i.e., to the cube).

Fire and air and water which have (only) three (factors)—I mean matter and form and that by which there is /21/ uniform motion with respect to place—(were ascribed) to that which is enclosed by triangles (i.e., to the tetrahedron, octahedron, and icosahedron). The sky, which possesses five (factors)—I mean matter and form, [60: 1] and that by which there is uniform motion with respect to place, and stability of state, and intelligent action—(was ascribed) to that which is enclosed by pentagons (i.e., to the dodecahedron).

(Fire, Air, Water—Second Consideration) [33]

/2/ Because fire is the first of them (i.e., of the mundane elements) and the finest of them, there was ascribed to it that of the figures which is first in the number of bases and the sharpest and the finest of them, /3/ I mean the (solid) which has four bases. And there was attributed to that which (follows it) in the order (of the mundane elements) and in fineness—I mean air— /4/ (the solid) which follows the one with four bases in the number of bases and in fineness and sharpness of the angles, I mean the (solid) which has eight /5/ bases. To the last one of them (i.e., the mundane elements) in the order and in fineness—I mean water—there was attributed (the solid) which has the most bases and (also) the most /6/ and the largest angles, I mean the (solid) which has twenty bases.

[32] Reading *dhū* for *ilā*.
[33] This section is wholly redundant with 57: 6-11 above. It adds nothing new and seems to be present only to preserve the symmetry of the discussion.

(*The Celestial Sphere—Second Consideration*)

/7/ Many of the ancients ascribed the sky to the quintuple because they saw that /8/ everything created by God that is in the sky has sense and intelligence, whereas intelligence and sense are not general to everything upon the earth, /9/ but that which is general to them (all) is generation.[34]

(*Transition*)

/10/ Therefore reflect, my praiseworthy brother, how nature has indicated in this way that the cause of everything /11/ is a single one without any plurality, which does not depart from its (own proper) nature, and does not resemble any of its effects, (not even) by a subtle resemblance which is concealed /12/ from corporeal eyes but clear to intellectual insight.

(*Preeminence of the Sphere Over the Five Regular Solids*)

/13/ The spherical figure is contained within one single surface without any plurality, and does not depart from its (own proper) nature /14/ as a cause of existence. But as regards the first figures [35]— I mean those whose sides, angles, and bases are equal and similar /15/ since the regular ones are first, because the regular ones are natural and those removed from regularity (are such) accidentally and not naturally, /16/ and the natural is prior to its accidents— (they are such that) (or: *through*) the existence of the sphere there exists each one of the rest (of the figures).

Also, the sphere /17/ is not similar to any one of those which have surfaces, because it is not a manifold whereas they are manifold, and the lines /18/ that lie upon the figures which have bases are straight, whereas those which lie upon the sphere are altogether curved (i.e., are arcs), and it is impossible for one of them /19/ to be a straight line. Howsoever you cut a sphere by a single plane surface, their (resulting) divisions are all alike [61: 1] circles and nothing else. But the (solids) with bases (are such that) however you divide them by a single plane surface their (resulting) divisions are different (figures) /2/ and have sides.

---

[34] Cf. 59: 21–60: 1 above.
[35] That is, the regular solids.

(Furthermore) the sphere touches every (kind of) figure at the limit of one single boundary [36]—I mean one single mark /3/ without plurality—whereas the (solids) with bases meet the (various kinds of) figures in many fashions: either at the limit of a line, /4/ or at the limit of a surface, or at the limit of a body (volume). (Also) the sphere (is such that) all the lines which divide it into two halves (i.e., all its diameters) /5/ are of one single measure (i.e., length) without plurality and without diversity, whereas the (solids) with bases, (are such that) not all the lines that divide them /6/ into two halves (i.e., all the diameters) are of one single measure (i.e., length), but they are diverse and plural. (Also) the sphere (is such that) all the angles (from any given point) that touch (both) its surface and its diameter /7/ —(i.e.) a line that divides (it, i.e., the sphere) into two halves—are (all) equal and similar, I mean that they are stable (i.e., *uniform*) without diversity and plurality. But as to those (solids) that have /8/ bases, it is not the case that all angles that touch (both) their surfaces and diameter—(i.e.) a line that divides (them) into two halves—are (all) equal and /9/ similar, but (they are) diverse and plural.

Furthermore the sphere can set in motion everything that surrounds it /10/ and that touches it. But as to the figures that have bases, this is not possible for them. (Also) the motion of a sphere can /11/ be eternal and ceaseless, because it does not move from (one) place to (another) place, but (moves) in one single place, /12/ without plurality and change. But as to the motions of (bodies) other than spherical, this cannot be the case with them, for they move from (one) place to (another) place: [37] /13/ their places change and are plural. Therefore it is not possible that it (i.e., non-spherical motion) be eternal, because it is not possible that there be a /14/ place without (any) limits. As we have shown in many other discussions of ours, it is not possible that there be any actual thing that does not have limits.

(*Uniqueness of the Immaterial*)

/15/ Nature does not indicate solely the oneness (uniqueness of

---

[36] Reading *b-h-d-d* for *b-ʿ-d*.

[37] The text should read *min makān ilā makān* exactly as in the preceding line.

God, but in every divine completion, and especially [38] /16/ in everything devoid of matter, as are these figures which we have discussed. For the cause of the particularity [39] /17/ of every figure of the sensible-substances which have matter (i.e., of all material substance) is one single figure [40] without plurality, movable neither /18/ to a greater (i.e., increase) nor a lesser (i.e., diminution), nor a recipient of anything accidental.[41] Such are the sensible circles, some of which are larger than /19/ others, receiving through their matter many accidents, by way of color, position, motion, becoming and other [62: 1] accidents beside these. The cause and the genus of all of them is the single circle which has no matter and no accident and no /2/ motion towards the greater (or lesser), because the greater and the lesser both have existence only by the addition and with the extension of matter (in accordance with) its being more or less. /3/ Likewise, for every species of the remaining figures there is a single figure without motion and without plurality which is the cause of its existence.

/4/ The cause [42] of all the figures is one single thing, namely the form, I mean that by which a thing is what it is. /5/ Even thus, the cause of all enumerations is the One which is not plural in its nature and not divisible.

/6/ Similarly with all sensible-substances, the cause of their existence is their form which is general to them, such as a man, for it is by the form /7/ of manhood that he is what he is. And manhood and the other forms of animals are what they are by the form of animality.

/8/ Similarly with the living and the non-living, above them is substance, because it is by substance that they are what they are. And similarly /9/ all things are what they are by (the form of) whatness.

/10/ Thus all things come to a limit (or: *end*) as regards their causes in one single limit (or: *end*), I mean (in) one single cause, not several.

---

[38] Reading *lā sīman* for *wa sīman*.

[39] I.e., the *principium individuationis*.

[40] Here, and correspondingly at 62: 1, 3 below, " single " (*wāḥid*) is employed technically to indicate the Platonic idea, equated to the Aristotelian form at 62: 4.

[41] Reading *b-tt-h* for the *b-thth-h* of the printed text. Compare 62: 11 and 63: 4.

[42] Compare with the remainder of this section *Timaeus* 30c–31a.

(Cosmic and Divine Unity)

/11/ Thus nature has indicated in all things whatsoever that the cause of everything is one, true and not at all plural from any side (aspect); /12/ since every existence that has unity is [also] multiple from a side (aspect) other than the one that caused its existence. /13/ Some of these causes are less plural than others, as we have explained in our book entitled *Kitāb al-falsafah al-ūlā* (" Book on first philosophy (= metaphysics) ").[43] /14/ We have examples of this now. The spherical which is not plural from the aspect (side) of its surface and of /15/ all we have mentioned (above), is (nevertheless) plural in the number of things by every one of which it is (rendered) plural, which /16/ we enumerated above from the aspect (side) of its dimensions (literally: *distances*); for it has length, breadth, and depth, and it has parts.

/17/ Thus the cause of every existing unity that has plurality in one of its aspects, is the One (i.e., God) which is not plural /18/ in any aspect, since [44] that which brings about the cause for every one of the pluralities is one which has less plurality than it, [63: 1] as what we said before [45] in regard to particular things and the form ascending to whatness, [showing] that the causes end in /2/ one single cause. For (their) number ends in its decrease to one, because every cause, since it has less plurality /3/ than its effects is thereby nearer to true unity than its effect.

/4/ Thus the cause of the cause that has least plurality has (itself) no plurality at all: The cause of all is one single God. Plurality does not touch him in any /5/ aspect (or: *on any side*) nor does diminution, since he is touched neither by divisibility nor by decrease in any aspect at all.

(Closing)

/6/ Blessed is the Creator of all, the Sustainer of all, the Perfector of all, He who is hidden from [46] corporeal eyes.

---

[43] Also published in Abū Rīdah's collection of treatises by al-Kindī. On the idea of a hierarchy of causes, such that as one proceeds from the lower to the higher there is increasingly less plurality until one reaches the True One (*al-wāḥid al-haqq*) see M. E. Marmura and J. M. Rist, " Al-Kindī's Discussions of Divine Existence and Oneness," *Mediaeval Studies*, vol. 25 (1963), pp. 338–354.

[44] Suppressing the *huwa* of the printed text.

[45] See 62: 8–9.

[46] Reading *ʿinda* for *ʿan-hu.*

/7/ The treatise is completed. Praise be to God, Lord of all the worlds, and may His blessings be upon His Prophet Muḥammad and his people.[47]

---

[47] I am most grateful to Prof. M. E. Marmura of the University of Toronto for checking my translation and eliminating some infelicities from it.

III
YAḤYĀ IBN ʿADĪ'S TREATISE
"ON THE FOUR SCIENTIFIC QUESTIONS
REGARDING THE ART OF LOGIC"

A. Introduction

1. Yaḥyā ibn ʿAdī

Abū Zakariyyā' Yaḥyā ibn ʿAdī ibn Ḥamīd (893-974) was one of
the greatest of the series of important Arab-Christian theologian-
philosophers of the 9th-11th centuries.[1] He was born in Takrit
(Iraq) in 893, of Monophysite Christian parentage, and studied
medicine, theology, science, and philosophy in Baghdad. The great
al-Fārābī, as well as his teacher Abū Bishr Mattā ibn Yūnus, were
among his teachers, and he is also reported to have studied medicine
and logic with the Rhazes.[2] He settled in Baghdad where he lived
the rest of his life, earning his livelihood as a physician and as a
teacher of philosophy. Although he wrote extensively on (Christian)

---

[1] For this author, the following sources should be consulted: Brockelmann,
GAL: I (1), p. 207; I (2), p. 228; SI, pp. 370, 956; Georg Graf, " Die Philosophie
und Gotteslehre des Jaḥyā ibn ʿAdī," *Beiträge zur Geschichte der Philosophie des
Mittelalters*, VIII, pt. 7 (Münster, 1910); G. Furlani, " Le ʿ Questioni Filosofiche '
di Abū Zakariyā Yaḥyā b. ʿAdī," *Rivista degli Studi Orientali*, vol. 8 (1919-1920),
pp. 157-162; L. Cheikho, *Vingt Traités Théologiques d'Auteurs Arabes Chrétiens*
(2d ed., Beirut, 1920); Augustin Périer, *Yaḥyā ben ʿAdī: Un Philosophe Arabe
Chrétien du Xe Siècle* (Paris, 1920); Max Meyerhof, " Von Alexandrien nach
Baghdad," *Sitzungsberichte der Preussischen Akademie der Wissenschaften* (Philosophisch-
historische Klasse) (Berlin, 1930), pp. 417-421; Georg Graf, *Geschichte der Christlich
Arabischen Literatur* (Rome, 1937-1938; *Studi e Testi*), vol. II, pp. 233-240; George
Sarton, *Introduction to the History of Science*, vol. I (Baltimore, 1927), pp. 629-630;
N. Rescher, *The Development of Arabic Logic* (Pittsburgh, 1964), pp. 130-134.
[2] Meyerhof, *op. cit.*, pp. 417-421.

theological subjects, it was as a teacher of philosophy that he made his greatest impact. ʿĪsā ibn Zurʿah,[3] Abū Sulaimān al-Sijistānī,[4] Ibn al-Samḥ,[5] and Ibn al-Khammār (or Ibn Suwār)[6] were among his pupils. Yaḥyā ibn ʿAdī was a prolific copyist of manuscripts, and built up a considerable library by his own labors. More importantly, he prepared many excellent translations of Greek works from Syriac into Arabic. In 974 Yaḥyā ibn ʿAdī died in Baghdad at an advanced age.

Yaḥyā ibn ʿAdī was concerned especially with logic; he was dubbed " the logician " (al-manṭiqī) because of his productivity in this field. He made Arabic translations, from Syriac, of most of the treatises of Aristotle's logical Organon, as well as of Greek commentaries upon them by Ammonius, Themistius, and Alexander of Aphrodisias. In addition to these translations, Yaḥyā ibn ʿAdī wrote a number of independent minor treatises on logical matters, one of which occupies us here.[7]

2. Yaḥyā ibn ʿAdī's Treatise

The work presently at issue is a short epistolary treatise entitled " On the four scientific questions regarding the art of logic." This treatise, whose existence was previously known by report, was recovered in an Istanbul manuscript[8] and was published by the Turkish orientalist Mlle Mubahat Türker in 1956.[9] An English translation of this treatise is given below. We shall first offer some preliminary observations.

First and foremost, the treatise by Yaḥyā ibn ʿAdī " On the four scientific questions regarding the art of logic " is a piece of *propaganda for logic* and an apology for the study of the subject. In this respect

---

[3] Brockelmann, GAL, SI, pp. 377, 427, 435.
[4] *Ibid.*, I, p. 208.
[5] S. M. Stern, " Ibn al-Samḥ," *Journal of the Royal Asiatic Society*, 1956, pp. 31–44.
[6] Brockelmann, GAL, I, p. 328.
[7] For the details of our author's literary activity, see particularly Périer, *op. cit.*
[8] Aya Sofya, MS no. 4818.
[9] " Yaḥyā ibn ʿAdī ve Nesredilmemis, bir Risalesi," *Ankara Üniversitesi Dil ve Tarih-Goğrafya Fakültesi Dergisi*, vol. 14 (1956), pp. 87–102. Mlle Türker also gives a Turkish translation which regrettably had to be ignored by us, due to ignorance of Turkish. However, see notes 11–14 and 16–19 below for proposed corrections in the published Arabic text. No reference is made here to what one can safely assume to be merely typographical errors.

his treatise is closely comparable with his pupil ʿĪsā ibn Zurʿah's " Treatise on the Innocence of Those Who Inquire into Logic and Philosophy." [10] Like his pupil, Yaḥyā ibn ʿAdī is concerned to elucidate the true nature of logic in order to establish the propriety of logical study and the need for logic as a means to the good, to happiness, and even to salvation. (It is interesting to note that the prefatory rubric anticipates the title of Maimonides' great work, stating the title of the treatise as: " Guidance for Those Who Are Lost to the Path of Salvation.") The author's lament that many people question or even deny the usefulness of logic sets the stage for his discussion.

The " four scientific questions about logic " concern (i) its existence (*hal hiya*; *anniyyah*), (ii) its general nature (*mā hiya*; *māhiyyah*), (iii) its specific character (*ayy shayʾ hiya*; *ayyiyyah*), and (iv) its use (*limā hiya*; *limayyah*).[11] (It is clearly the last item, the usefulness of logic, that is uppermost in our author's mind.) The enumeration of the " four scientific questions " acquires special importance in the light of Avicenna's systematic discussion of the logic of questions to be dealt with in the next chapter. For Yaḥyā ibn ʿAdī's treatment of the matter provides strong presumptive evidence that the entire theory of questions with which Avicenna deals is part of the standard machinery of the Arabic logical tradition.

One of the most interesting features of the treatise is the long digression on the " pathology of error " in reasoning, almost half of the discourse being devoted to an analysis of the sources of error in thought, illustrated with various bio-medical analogies. In part this may reflect the intimate link between logic and medicine in Yaḥyā ibn ʿAdī's milieu, and indeed through the entire " logico-medical " tradition from Galen to Avicenna. On the other hand it is clear that our author's view of logic as the " medicine of the mind " constitutes for him perhaps the strongest argument on its behalf.

[10] See N. Rescher, " A Tenth-Century Arab-Christian *Apologia* for Logic," *Studies in the History of Arabic Logic* (Pittsburgh, 1963), pp. 55–63. The Arabic text of this treatise, uniquely extant in a Paris MS, was published by this author under the same title in *Islamic Studies* (Journal of the Central Institute of Islamic Research, Karachi), vol. 2 (1963), pp. 1–16.

[11] A useful discussion of the four scientific questions can be found in A. Altmann and S. M. Stern, *Isaac Israeli* (London, 1958), pp. 10–23.

B. Translation of Yahyā ibn ʿAdī's Treatise
" On the Four Scientific Questions Regarding
the Art of Logic " [12]

[118 b] [13] A treatise by Yahyā ibn ʿAdī ibn Zakariyyāʾ on the four scientific questions regarding the art of logic. These are: whether it is, what it is, which thing it is, and why it is. He entitles it: " Guidance for Those Who Are Lost to the Path of Salvation." He said:

(Usefulness)

If the actions of all people agreed with their words in affirming the truth and following it, this would have made it unnecessary for us to have to undertake showing the excellence of the art of logic and its great usefulness, as the obviousness [of its value] is apparent with the easiest reflection. But since many people would deny this, and exert their effort in refuting it either out of ignorance or to be quarrelsome, it would be most necessary for us to open our discourse on this art by showing the definite good apprehendable by it and the benefit deriving from it. This would be more conducive to desiring it, and for bearing the hardships in seeking it.

All that is desired, preferred, and loved, is desired, preferred, and loved because it has some good in it, or [deriving] from it or by it, real or imagined. The good is of two kinds: *intrinsic* [or essential], [pertaining to] the things such that the good in them is in their essence, and is what is implied in their definition—as we shall show of the art of logic; and, *accidental*, which is the good that is accidental [to a thing], and chances to be in it or by it or from it, such as the falling of a stone on someone with an abscess and lancing it, leading to its healing. But [14] that whose good is intrinsic is better than that in which the good is accidental.

---

[12] Translated in collaboration with Professor Fadlou Shehadi.
[13] These numbers give the pagination of the Arabic manuscript as indicated in Mlle Türker's edition.
[14] Reading *wa-ʾamma* rather than *wa-ʾimma*.

(General Nature)

The benefit deriving from the art of logic is intrinsic not accidental, and this can be seen in its definition. It is *an instrumental art by which one discriminates between truth and falsehood in theoretical science, and between good and evil in practical science.* The remoteness of the meanings of the terms which we used in its [i.e., logic's] definition from the understanding of many people requires us to explain what is in it [i.e., the definition] term by term, so that its meaning will be firmly established in the self.

An " art " is an ability of the self to act on an object out of thought and deliberation toward some purpose. " Instrumental " (" *adawiyyah* ") derives from " *adāt* " (tool) and *adāt* is an instrument intermediary between the artisan and that which is made. By its means the artisan achieves the perfection of his art [in relation to] its object, and infuses its employment by rational discrimination. " Rational discrimination " is the extraction [119 a] of what is common to things which differ from one another. " The true " is the reality of what is and of what pertains to it; it is what is. " The false " is what contradicts the reality of what is, what is not what is. " Science " is the apprehension of the reality of the things that are by virtue of which they are. " Theoretical " (" *nazharī* ") derives from " *nazhar* " (lit. " seeing," or " sight "), and *nazhar* is an investigation the ultimate aim of which is the apprehension of the reality of that which is inquired into. [Thus] a theoretical [science] is a science the ultimate aim of which is the apprehension of the reality of things. " Practical " derives from " practice," and practice is the acquisition of an object [objective] formally [i.e., with respect to its form]. The practical [science] is a science the ultimate aim of which is bringing about the good and avoidance of evil. This is the explanation of the terms used.

(Usefulness Again)

It has become apparent from what we said, first, that the good is intrinsic [to logic] since it is understood in its definition and by it is its subsistence. It has become apparent, moreover, that the good obtained by it and apprehended by its means is beyond any parallel, since it [i.e., this good] is complete happiness. There is no happiness more complete for theory than belief in the truth, and it is through it [i.e., logic] that this is apprehended; and none for practice more complete than acquiring the good, which without it [logic] cannot be possessed.

(Existence and Specific Character)

As to the existence of a science with such description, it will be apparent from what I say now that [15] everything known is known either (1) without resorting to it [i.e., logic], from a knowledge of something else, and without the need to make an inference about it [i.e., the known thing] from a knowledge of something preceding it—so that it is known by itself. This [i.e., the " known by itself "] is of two kinds.

(i) The first is material and perceivable. This is either composed of matter and form—and its essence is its form—and its becoming known is the occurrence of its form in the self without its matter. Or, what is accidental to the composite of matter and form; this is either with the possibility that the self can imagine its [the object's] form in its [the object's] absence, just as we imagine what we perceived of the buildings of one of the cities when we are in another city. This is called *imagination*. Or, without the possibility for the self to have an image of it except in its presence. This imagining [image-having] is called *perception*.

(ii) The other kind is formal but not material, and it is obtained through reason. Its kinds are generally called *first principles of reason* which cannot be proved. It is of two sorts: simple, especially called assigning [meaning] and defining; and composite, especially called axiomatic knowledge, and premisses without a middle term, and [other] matters it is necessary to accept.

Or, (2) [the knowledge] is obtained by resorting to it [i.e., logic] from a knowledge of things other than it, [for] in its exploration [logic] requires preceding knowledge. This kind of exploration is called inference, syllogism, [119 b] and proof.

As to the existence of the first two kinds [i.e., materially perceptible knowledge (perception and imagination) and formal non-material

---

[15] Reading *'anna* instead of *'inna*.

knowledge (non-inferential reason)], that is too obvious to need any attempt to establish it. As to this third kind [i.e., inferential knowledge], its existence may be seen from the arts and the sciences, for the knowledge of these continues to increase and multiply. The geometricians always derive properties and necessary attributes from the properties of lines, planes, bodies, and their necessary attributes which they did not know beforehand. Similarly, the arithmeticians derive from the properties of numbers what they [i.e., the arithmeticians] did not have [before]. Their method in this is by deriving what they did not have from what they had known previously and acquired in themselves, in matters of magnitude and numbers. This suffices in demonstrating the existence of this kind of exploration.

(Digression on the Sources of Error)

What is plain is that by each one of these kinds [of sources of knowledge]—I mean reason, perception, and thought, [thought] being the power by which inference comes about—what is apprehended, is apprehended as it really is, only if it [i.e., the faculty] is in a state of health and freedom from the corrupting infirmities which make it fail in its purpose. The senses perceive their sensibles, and the power of imagination imagines what it imagines, as they really are only if they [i.e., the senses and imagination] are healthy, with no infirmity in them. [Similarly] reason grasps the intelligibles in their reality only if it is free from damage. And the power of thought apprehends what is inferred as it is only if the method resorted to is correct and if it [i.e., thought] is, besides, healthy and sound. But if the senses and the power of imagination are infirm, then it is possible to perceive what is perceived and imagined as in a different form, just as sight perceives white [as] black if its constitution is overcome by black bile [melancholy], perceives it yellow if it is overcome by yellow bile [choler]. And buzzing and ringing occur in one's hearing when [an external cause of] neither exists. [It is possible] to smell the stinking [as] perfumed and the perfumed [as] stinking; to taste the sweet bitter, the bitter sweet; to feel the rough soft, the soft rough; and to imagine that before one there are things visible or audible, or aught else of what is perceivable, when there is no reality to that. The same thing happens to reason if the instrument with which it does its work, the brain, is sick. Then its conceiving and what it conceives are corrupted.

Just as we are likely to find some people for whom first principles, so extremely apparent to reason, are remote from their understanding, such as our saying that the whole is greater than any of its parts, or that what is necessarily true of anything is either its affirmation or its negation, what opposes it, thus, also, one is [sometimes] compelled to move from known and apparent things to hidden things, along an unsound path. This is likely not to lead to [120 a] the truth of what is sought, nay its opposite. If someone took two true premises, as someone might say, " Every stone is a body," " Not one of the animals is a stone," and then arranged them and said, " Not one of the animals is a stone and every stone is a body," what would follow from both premises is, " Not one of the animals is a body." This is a falsehood, which [seemed] necessitated by two true premises. You must know that we have said it was necessary [but] according to opinion not in reality. For it is not necessary in reality. The falsehood emerged only from the bad arrangement of the two premises, not from them in themselves, for their truth is apparent.

You must know that the conditions of error that befall these kinds are not one condition but different ones. Thus of these [sources of knowledge] it is sufficient for reason to conceive the intelligibles as they actually are without [there being] weakness in the health of its instrument. But for perception this alone is not [16] enough, for it needs, besides, the combination of other things, since sight may be extremely healthy and [still] perceive sensible things not as they really are; just as the sun is perceived as big as a cubit, but according to what proof has established it is many times [the size of] the earth. The cause for this is its [i.e., the sun's] distance. Similarly the considerable proximity to sight of things seen is the cause for seeing them much larger in magnitude.[17] Also, reverberation can happen to the hearing even though it is extremely healthy and strong. [So] also the method of syllogism and its strength, [even] if these [i.e., the

[16] Reading *fa-lā* instead of *wa-lā*.
[17] Reading *miqdārihā* instead of *miqdārihi*.

method and strength] are extremely sound, may [still] lead to error if their obstacles are not removed for them. For, this syllogism which says, " If someone says, ' It is a stone,' he is saying, ' it is a substance ' "—that [inference] is valid. It has led to an obvious falsehood, even though the arrangement of this syllogism is a correct one, and its two premisses are true.[18] Therefore, besides being sound in strength and method, it [syllogistic inference] might be in need of careful reflection and thinking over of [that] part of the material of the syllogism which are the premisses, and bringing to the mind their meanings and their necessary attributes, [both] as single and as composite.

This is the difference between the method of inference [on the one hand] and perception and imagination [on the other]. Two things are sufficient for perception and imagination. These are: their health, and the occurrence [or presence] of the perceived or imagined, such that, or in a condition proper for perceiving and imagining it as [120 b] it is. As for the method of inference, these two are not sufficient for it. What is needed in addition is for the inferrer carefully to look into this [i.e., the inference], to reflect on it and examine [19] it thoroughly, so it will be safe from the occurrence of error.[20] Perhaps if one were to look carefully into this meaning, which we said is peculiar to the method of inference and not to perception and imagination, it would be found that there is universal agreement about it [i.e., the meaning], and [what we said] was found to be common to it. However, a close study [21] of this is beyond our purpose in this discourse, and going beyond it [i.e., our purpose] is out of place in [relation to] what we intended by it [i.e., the discourse]. Therefore, we must refrain from prolonging its explanation.

[18] The text is muddled at this point. What our author may have in mind is something like this. Consider the valid syllogism:

All stones are substances
X is a stone
—————————
X is a substance

If the premisses are supposed true, the conclusion follows. Yet someone could nevertheless *misunderstand* the conclusion, construing it to make the false claim " X is *merely* a substance, but not a man or a tree or a stone, etc."

[19] Reading *wa-taqaṣṣīh* instead of *wa-tafaṣṣīh*.

[20] Omitting the *al-* of *al-wuqūʿ* and the *min* before *al-khaṭaʾ*.

[21] Again reading *taqaṣṣī* instead of *tafaṣṣī*.

(*Conclusion*)

The existence of the art of logic has become apparent by what we said. The essential need for it has also been established, for without it there is no arriving at happiness, neither the theoretical nor the practical. Previously, it became apparent, what it is, and which thing it is. And these are the four scientific queries.

If this is the measure of its usefulness, how right it would be for us [22] to have desire for it, and to bear every difficulty and hardship in attaining it.

Completed is the discourse on the thatness, whatness, whichness, and whyness of the art of logic.[23]

---

[22] Reading *ahaqqanā* instead of *ahaqquhā*.

[23] The pious invocations at the beginning and end of the treatise, obviously added by the Muslim scribe, have been omitted in translation.

IV

AVICENNA ON THE LOGIC OF QUESTIONS

In the past few years the Logic of Questions has come into its own as a branch of logical theory which has generated widespread interest and has been extensively cultivated.[1] It is thus germane to call attention to the (relatively brief) treatment of the theory of questions by the famous Persian-Arabic philosopher Avicenna (980–1037).[2]

In several of his logical treatises, Avicenna takes up the task of providing an analysis and a systematic classification of questions.[3] The upshot of his attempts to provide a classification of questions is presented in Table I.

---

[1] A pioneer work of the recent discussions is M. and A. Prior, " Erotetic Logic," *The Philosophical Review*, vol. 64 (1955), pp. 43–59. Three important monographs are: D. Harrah, *Communication: A Logical Model* (Cambridge, Mass., 1963); N. D. Belnap, Jr., *An Analysis of Questions: Preliminary Report* (Santa Monica, 1963); L. Aqvist, *A New Approach to the Logical Theory of Interrogatives*, pt. I (Uppsala, 1965). For a brief but synoptic discussion see the article " Questions " by C. L. Hamblin in P. Edwards (ed.), *The Encyclopedia of Philosophy*, vol. VII (New York, 1967), pp. 49–53.

[2] On Avicenna as a logician see N. Rescher, *The Development of Arabic Logic* (Pittsburgh, 1964), especially pp. 149–155.

[3] Our principal sources are: (1) *Dānesh-nāme*, anonymously edited in Tehran in 1331 A.H. (= 1912); tr. by M. Achena and H. Massé, *Avicenne: Le Livre de Science*, vol. I, Sections on logic and metaphysics (Paris, 1955), pp. 84–85; (2) *Kitāb al-ishārāt wa-' l-tanbīhāt*, ed. J. Forget (Leiden, 1982); ed. with the commentary of Nāṣir al-Dīn al-Ṭūsī (b. 1201) by S. Dunyā (Cairo, 1960); tr. A. M. Goichon, *Livres des Directives et Remarques* (Paris, 1951); see pp. 85–86 of the Forget text and pp. 234–238 of the translation; (3) *Kitāb al-najāt*, ed. M. Kurdī (Cairo, 1938); the material on questions is extracted and translated in a series of footnotes on pp. 235–237 of A. M. Goichon, *op. cit.*

Table I

Avicenna's Classification of Questions

Basic Questions (muṭālib umhāt)

1. The *is-it* question (*hal al-shay'*)
   i. Re. existence *simply* (*mawjūd muṭlaqan*)
   ii. Re. existence *in-a-state* (*mawjūd bi-ḥāl kadhā*)
2. The *what-is-it* question (*mā al-shay'*)
   i. Re. essence-of-the-thing (*dhāt al-shay'*)
      [a] definition (*ḥadd*)
      [b] description (*rasm*)
   ii. Re. meaning-of-the-word (*mafhūm al-ism*)
3. The *what-sort* question (*ayyu al-shay'*)
   (Re. the genus, species, and difference of the thing)
4. The *why* question (*limā al-shay'*)
   i. Why *is*: the cause (the four causes: [a] material, [b] formal, [c] efficient, [d] final)
   ii. Why *said*: the reason

Subsidiary Questions (muṭālib juz'iyyah)

5. The *how* question (*kayfa al-shay'*)
6. The *where* question (*ayna al-shay'*)
7. The *when* question (*matā al-shay'*)
8. The *how-much* question (*kammiyyat al-ashyā'*) [4]

The principal distinctions involved in this classification are as follows:

1. *Basic questions vs. subsidiary questions.* The rationale here appears to be that a basic question is one regarding the *existence*, the *nature*, and the *causes* of a thing: and thus deal with (a) questions concerning *substance* (rather than " accidents," in the sense of Aristotelian categories other than substance), plus (b) questions concerning the *causes* (which are extra-categorial questions). By contrast, the subsidiary questions deal with accidental features. Apparently this is the reason why Avicenna designates [5] the four basic questions (1–4) as the *scientific* questions, dealing with matters of essence and existence, and characterizes the subsidiary questions (5–8) as *non-scientific*, dealing with the accidental features of things. According to

---

[4] Listed in the *Dānesh-nāme*, but omitted in the *Ishārāt*.
[5] *Le Livre de Science*, vol. I, p. 84.

the Aristotelian view, science deals with the essential features of things—a scientific knowledge of accidents is accordingly impossible.

2. *Questions of fact vs. questions of discourse.* Avicenna is clear and explicit in distinguishing consideration of the nature of things from those regarding the meanings of words (2 i vs. 2 ii), and in distinguishing considerations as to why things *are* as they are from those regarding why things *are spoken of* as they are (4 i vs. 4 ii).[6] It would seem that Avicenna's pointed formulation of the matter represents a decisive step towards the later distinction between nominal and real definition.

3. *The priority of questions.* The idea operative here is that it can prove infeasible to raise a question Q_1 (e.g., that regarding the *purpose* of a thing) if a certain answer to another Question Q_2 (e.g., that regarding the existence of the thing) is not forthcoming. Avicenna consequently maintains, for example, that the *why* question (4 i) is posterior to the *is-it* question (1 i). In such a case—when the *legitimacy of raising* the question Q_1 turns on the obtaining of an appropriate (affirmative or negative) answer to Q_2—question Q_2 is said to have priority over Q_1. In just sense, the question " Is X an *accomplished* flutist? " would be posterior to the question " Does X play the flute at all? ": if the second is answered negatively, it would be pointless to raise the first.

* * *

It is necessary to note that Avicenna's treatment of the theory of questions is not original with him. For example, his treatment of the " four scientific questions " agrees in detail with Yaḥyā ibn 'Adī's discussion presented in the preceding chapter. This point of agreement between these two opponents shows that Avicenna's treatment of the logic of questions altogether reflects earlier Arabic logical tradition.[7]

It might seem at first blush that Avicenna's tabulation of questions was arrived at as a merely grammatical exercise, by simply compiling the interrogative particles of the Arabic language, the equivalents

[6] This distinction too comes from Aristotle. See *Metaphysics* Ƶ iv, 1030a 27–28. Cf. also *ibid.*, 1029b 13 and *Posterior Analytics* 92b 6–8, 26.

[7] In fact, the four questions are already to be found in al-Kindī. See A. Altmann and J. M. Stern, *Isaac Israeli* (London, 1958), p. 11.

of *what, why, how, where, when,* and the like. But this conception is mistaken, and loses sight of the venerable and august ancestry of the venture. For *Avicenna's tabulation of questions is in fact derived from Aristotle's categories,* duly augmented by the five predicables of Porphyry. There can be no doubt of this, in the face not only of the parallelism of the concepts at work here, but also the close correspondence of the Arabic terminology at issue in the discussion of categories.[8] The relevant data are assembled in Table II.

Table II
The Correspondence between the Aristotelian Categories,
the Porphyrean Predicables, and Avicenna's Questions

Category/ Predicable	Greek Name	Arabic Name	Question at Issue	Avicenna's Question
1. substance	οὐσία	al-jawhar	what thing?	(1i), (1ii) *
2. quantity	ποσόν	al-kammiyah	how much?	(8)
3. quality	ποιόν	ayyu	what sort?	(3)
i. genus	γένος	jins		
ii. species	εῖδος	naw'		
iii. difference	διαφορά	faṣl		
iv. essential qualities	ἴδιον	dhāt	what nature?	(2 i)
—definitive	ὅρος	ḥadd		
—descriptive**	ὑπογραφη	rasm		
v. accidents	συμβεβηκότα	kayfa	how functioning?	(5)
4. relation	πρός τι	al-iḍāfah	how related?	
7. posture	κεῖσθαι	waḍ'	in what attitude?	
8. possession	ἔχειν	lahu	with what accompaniments?	nothing
9. action	ποιεῖν	an yaf'al	what doing?	
10. passion	πάσχειν	an yuf'al	what undergoing?	
5. place	ποῦ	ayna	where?	(6)
6. time	ποτε	matā	when?	(7)
(11. cause ***	αἰτία	al-sabab	why?	(4))

Annotations
* Roughly, the two parts of this question ask regarding the primary and secondary substance at issue, respectively.
** Regarding this entry, see footnote 15 below.
*** Regarding this 11th entry see the discussion in the text.

[8] Cf. D. M. Dunlop, " Al-Fārābī's Paraphrase of the *Categories* of Aristotle," *The Islamic Quarterly,* vol. 4 (1958), pp. 168–197; vol. 5 (1959), pp. 21–54.

Two aspects of this tabulation should be noted especially:

1. It helps to bring out quite clearly the fact that Avicenna approaches questions from an *ontological* direction, viewing them all as questions asked about *an existing thing* (this was already implicit in the Arabic nomenclature), and that this thing is to be considered in isolation (hence we drop reference to the category of relation as well as its cognates posture and possession), and without regard to other things by which it may be affected or upon which it might be acting (hence we drop reference to the categories of action and passion).[9]

2. For the completion of the correspondence we must however introduce—as a category?—the rubric of causation, which the important role of *why?* questions endows with special prominence.[10]

The introduction of *why?* questions has nothing to do with the elementary ontological analysis of the *Categories* but is required by the deeper analysis of *science*: to know a thing is to know its causes. Avicenna (in discussing demonstrative syllogism) *begins* with the analysis of questions in *An. Post.* II, *i* and fills it out by further use of the *Categories*.   One must regard the *what-sort?* question as somehow derived from Aristotle's question ὅτι: "that it is the case."[11]   For then the four Basic Questions coincide exactly with Aristotle's four " subjects for inquiry " [*loc. cit.*].   The process of their transmission can be traced through the Alexandrian Aristotelians to the Arabs in considerable detail.[12]

Was the passage from categories (plus predicables) to questions a transitional step which originated with the Arabs, rather than one

[9] In view of Avicenna's occasional dependence on Stoic sources, it is worth noting that his treatment of questions is clearly based on the Aristotelian doctrine of categories, in contrast to the simplified *Kategorienlehre* of the Stoics, for which see E. Zeller, *Die Philosophie der Griechen*, vol. III, pt. I, 5th ed. (*curavit* E. Wellman Leipzig, 1923; photoprinted Hildesheim, 1963), pp. 93–105. Thus the questions *is-it? what-is-it? why?* come straight out of *Posterior Analytics*, II, *i*; while the Stoic doctrine is entirely different, with no place for *what? where? when? how much?* etc.

[10] The theory of questions has an intimate relationship with the theory of demonstration, which deals with the establishment of answers.   (Note that Avicenna's treatment of questions falls into the section on demonstration.) Regarding this kinship (particularly with respect to *why?* questions) see M. E. Marmura, " Ghazali and Demonstrative Science," *Journal of the History of Philosophy*, vol. 3 (1965), pp. 183–204 (see especially pp. 190–191).

[11] Cf. A. M. Goichon, *op. cit.*, p. 236, n. 2.

[12] See Altmann and Stern, *Isaac Israeli* (*op. cit.*), pp. 13–14.

which had already been taken earlier, with the Greeks ? I cannot answer this question with absolute assurance, but I strongly suspect that the answer is negative. I base my conjecture on purely circumstantial evidence. It is a well-established fact that most of the departures made by Avicenna in logic from orthodox Aristotelian positions trace back to ultimately Stoic sources. And it is readily established that the Stoic logicians interested themselves in the logic of questions. For example Diogenes Laertius reports in his register of the logical works of Chrysippus (280–209 B.C.) that this important Stoic logician wrote an entire series of treatises on the logical theory of questions.[13] A meager modicum of information about this Stoic theory of questions is provided in sources available to us,[14] but this is unfortunately wholly insufficient to throw any light on the conjecture under discussion. None the less, it seems to me likely, all considered, that Avicenna's treatment of the logic of questions is (ultimately) indebted to the Stoic discussions on the subject. To be sure, the reference to " description " is the only point in Avicenna's classification of questions which, taken in isolation, is clearly Stoic and post-Aristotelian.[15] But the tactic of realigning categorial ideas around the organizing theme of questions seems to me to have the earmarks of a Stoic innovation.[16]

---

[13] *Peri erōteseōs* (" On Questions ": 2 books), *Peri peuseōs* (" On Queries ": 4 books), *Epitomē peri erōteseōs kai peuseōs* (" Epitome on Questions and Queries "), *Peri apokriseōs* (" On Answers ": 4 books), *Epitomē peri apokriseōs* (" Epitome on Answers "). See Diogenes Laertius, *Lives of the Eminent Philosophers*, VII: 191 (ed. D. H. Hicks in the Loeb series, vol. II, p. 300). A *question* (*erōtēma*) can be answered yes or no (e.g., " Is today Monday? "); a *query* (*pysma*) is an interrogation that cannot be so answered (e.g., " What day is it? "). (*Ibid.*, VII: 66.) Compare B. Mates, *Stoic Logic* (Berkeley, 1953), pp. 18–19.

[14] See C. Prantl, *Geschichte der Logik im Abendlande*, vol. I (Leipzig, 1855; photo-reprinted Graz, 1955), p. 441, n. 115.

[15] The term " description " (*hypographē*) is not used by Aristotle, but was first used by the Stoics, and came to the Arabic philosophers *via* Galen and the Alexandrian commentators. See Altmann and Stern, *Isaac Israeli* (*op. cit.*), pp. 10–11 (n. 1).

[16] I wish to thank Mr. Neil A. Gallagher for affording me assistance in compiling and evaluating some of the data presented in this chapter. And I am grateful to Professor Charles H. Kahn for helpful suggestions and constructive criticisms.

V

IBN AL-ṢALĀḤ ON ARISTOTLE ON CAUSATION

A. INTRODUCTION

1. Ibn al-Ṣalāḥ

Abū 'l-Futūḥ Aḥmad ibn Muḥammad ibn al-Surā Najm al-Dīn ibn al-Ṣalāḥ was born in Persia around 1090.[1] He flourished in Baghdad, where he became an influential physician. He died in 1153.

In his scholarly work, Ibn al-Ṣalāḥ wrote primarily on scientific subjects, especially mathematics and astronomy. Apart from the (incomplete) treatise presented here, only one of the dozen of Ibn al-Ṣalāḥ's surviving treatises has to date received attention, his treatise " On the Fourth Figure of the Assertoric Figures [of the Syllogism] Attributed to Galen." [2]   In these two treatises, Ibn al-Ṣalāḥ reveals himself as a highly competent scholar, of distinctively mathematical orientation and with an unusually keen interest in the historico-bibliographical side of his subject.

2. The Istanbul Codex and the Present Treatise

In 1936 the late German Arabist Max Krause published a report on Islamic mathematical manuscripts he had examined in Istanbul

---

[1] On this scholar's life and work see C. Brockelmann, *Geschichte der Arabischen Litteratur*, vol. I (2d ed., Leiden, 1943), p. 621, entry (4c); *Supplement*, vol. I (Leiden, 1937), p. 857; H. Suter, *Die Mathematiker und Astronomen der Araber und ihre Werke* (Leipzig, 1900), p. 120, entry 287; N. Rescher, *The Development of Arabic Logic* (Pittsburgh, 1964), pp. 173–174; N. Rescher, *Galen and the Syllogism* (Pittsburgh, 1966).

[2] The treatise is edited, translated, and studied in N. Rescher, *Galen and the Syllogism* (*op. cit.*). See also A. I. Sabra, " A Twelfth-Century Defence of the Fourth Figure of the Syllogism," *Journal of the Warburg and Courtauld Institutes*, vol. 28 (1965), pp. 14–28.

in the course of a research visit during the winter of 1933–34.[3] In this report, Krause described a manuscript collection of treatises (rasā'il) by Ibn al-Ṣalāḥ in the possession of the Aya Sofya library in Istanbul.[4] The Aya Sofya codex contains eight treatises by Ibn al-Ṣalāḥ, all but two of which deal with points of Elucidean geometry. Of the other two, one deals with the fourth figure of the categorical syllogism.[5] The remaining part of the manuscript contains (the uniquely extant copy of) Ibn al-Ṣalāḥ's treatise entitled " Commentary on the End of the Second Book of Aristotle's Posterior Analytics, and the Correction of an Error in it " (Sharḥ faṣl fī akhir al-maqālat al-thāniyyah min kitāb Arisṭūṭātis fī 'l-burhān). Unfortunately the text of the treatise as given in the Aya Sofya codex (folios 158b–160a) is incomplete.[6] It stops in midstream and contains perhaps somewhat over half of the treatise. The presentation of this Arabic text, its translation into English, and the critical assessment of its contents is the aim which the present chapter has set for itself.[7]

3. Analysis of the Treatise

The subject of Ibn al-Ṣalāḥ's tract is the passage of Posterior Analytics, Book II (99a17–22) where Aristotle expounds the reciprocal relation of cause, subject of causation, and effect. The issue is conceived in terms of a " causal syllogism " of the form AAA–1 (Barbara). Such a syllogism takes the form

$$
\begin{array}{l}
\text{All } M \text{ is } P \\
\underline{\text{All } S \text{ is } M} \\
\text{All } S \text{ is } P
\end{array}
$$

Here the middle term (M) is the cause, the major term (P) is " that which has the cause," that is, the effect, and the minor term (S) is " the thing on which the cause operates," the subject of causation.

[3] " Stambuler Handschriften islamischer Mathematiker," Quellen und Studien zur Geschichte der Mathematik, Astronomie, und Physik, Abteilung B/Studien, vol. 3 (1936), pp. 437–532.
[4] Aya Sofya codex 4830.
[5] See N. Rescher, Galen and the Syllogism (op. cit.).
[6] This is not noted in Krause's description, op. cit., p. 486, entry no. 10.
[7] I am grateful to the authorities of the Aya Sofya Museum both for furnishing me with a microfilm of the Ibn al-Ṣalāḥ manuscript, and for affording me the opportunity to work with the manuscript itself during a visit to Istanbul in September, 1964.

The principal example is the syllogism:

> All plane regular polygons have exterior angles summing to
>   four right angles
> All triangles [squares, etc.] are plane regular polygons
> ———————————————————————————
> All triangles [squares, etc.] have exterior angles summing to
>   four right angles

Here then, *triangles* are the subject of causation, *having exterior angles summing to four right angles* is the effect, and *being a plane regular polygon* is the cause.

The first thesis is that these three items, in general, " are mutually necessary, and none of them is superior to the others " (158b12). In some cases, however, Aristotle is held to maintain that the cause " is superior " to the subject of causation. The bulk of the treatise is devoted to giving an exposition and justification of this contention.

The principal difficulty is that sometimes—the previous syllogism is an example—the subject of causation (S-term) is narrower in extension than the effect (P-term). Then the subject can be widened (as we have indicated in square brackets) until subject and effect become co-extensive. This point is argued at great length, following through on Aristotle's employment of a geometrical example. It is clear that Ibn al-Ṣalāḥ is fascinated by this geometrical example for he follows it up in the greatest detail (158b19–159b4), setting forth two distinct lines of proof for the geometrical fact at issue. Only after this analysis is completed—and this seems to be the main object of our mathematician author—do we return (briefly) to the exposition of Aristotle.

It is then (159b11–17) that we come to the *error* mentioned in the title of our treatise which, as it turns out, is not an error of Aristotle's at all, but a very minor slip in the Arabic translation, perhaps only on the part of the *copyist* of the translation.

The principal area of interest of the treatise is the clear light it throws upon the interpretation of the Arabic philosophers of Aristotle's theory of causation. The Master's syllogistic treatment of the matter was clearly bent by Avicenna in the direction of the Arabic logicians' analysis of *why?*-questions.[8] Once again, Aristo-

---

[8] See ch. IV above.

telian teachings come to be regarded in the school of Avicenna from the direction of conceptions of Stoic origins.

Finally a word about the light our treatise casts upon the mind of its author. He once again appears in the light of a careful student of texts, who carefully sifts the writings of the later authorities with a critical view to the faithfulness of their interpretations of the texts. His prime preoccupation with mathematics notwithstanding, Ibn al-Ṣalāḥ had something of the scholar's penchant for the comprehensive and accurate sifting of the historical data.

4. *Some Points of Mechanics*

The remaining two parts of this chapter will present Ibn al-Ṣalāḥ's treatise on the basis of the manuscript already mentioned (Aya Sofya 4830, folios 158b–160a). Part C presents a transcription of the manuscript, the numbering of pages and lines being indicated by a marginal index. Part B contains a (rather literal) annotated English translation of the text.[9] Here we have placed parentheses () around explanatory *elaborations* of the existing text, and brackets [] around explanatory *additions* to the text. The division into paragraphs is, in most instances, without manuscript warrant and is indicated by the sense of the discussion alone. Even the division into sentences is, as any Arabist knows, in some measure arbitrary. To facilitate reference and cross reference, the correlation of the translation with the text is indicated by a marginal index, the transition from line to line being shown by a vertical line |. For grammatical reasons this division cannot but be occasionally imperfect.

B. Translation

⟩ 1   In the name of God, the compassionate, the merciful
          With the aid of God, may He be praised.

2   " A commentary on a chapter at the end of the second book of
3 Aristotle's *Liber de demonstratione* (*Posterior Analytics*) | and the correction of an error in it." by the shaikh Abū 'l-Futūḥ Aḥmad ibn Muḥammad ibn al-Surā [ibn al-Ṣalāḥ], may God rest his soul.

[9] I should like to thank Salwa (Mrs. Souren) Teghrarian for helping with the transcription of the manuscript and also with the translation. Also, I am grateful to Mary (Mrs. Edward M.) Arnett for reading the proofs of the Arabic text.

4 | Aristotle said at the end of the second book of his *Liber de demonstratione* (*Posterior Analytics*) in the translation of Abū Bishr
5 Mattā ibn | Yūnus al-Qunānī [i.e., al-Qunāwī]:
The cause, and the thing on which the cause [operates] [i.e., the subject], and the thing which has the cause [i.e., the effect], are
6 all necessary for each other.[10] | The case here is as follows: If you
7 take the thing on which the cause [operates] only in part, then | it [i.e., the cause] is the greater. An example of this is [the term] " exterior angles equal to four right angles," which is greater [in applicability] than what pertains [solely] to the triangle and the
8 square. But | if you take all of them together [i.e., all the things which the cause operates], then they are equal; and this is so in all
9 things (i.e., figures) [11] whose exterior angles [12] | are equal to four right angles. The middle [term] is uniform [in the two premisses].[13]
The commentary on this [passage] is that he means that the
10 cause, which is | the middle term of the syllogism; [14] and the caused thing, namely that which he called " the thing which has the cause " [i.e., the effect], is the predicate term [i.e., the major]
11 | in the syllogism [viz. " having exterior angles summing to four right angles "], and the subject, namely the subject term in the syllogism [i.e., the minor] [viz. " triangles " or " squares " etc.],
12 is what he called " the thing on which | the cause [operates]."
The three of these are mutually necessary, and none of them is superior to the others.
13 But if we take certain species of subjects, | then the cause is superior to it [i.e., to the subject, " the thing on which the cause (operates) "]. This is the meaning of his statement:

---

[10] These are the three terms (middle, major, minor, respectively) of the " causal syllogism." Cf. the example of n. 5 below.
[11] See the margin of the MS here and also at 159b11.
[12] The text reads: " whose *four* exterior angles." But the " four " is unwanted here. Cf. 159b11–17 below.
[13] *Posterior Analytics*, II, xvii: 99a17–22.
[14] The syllogism at issue goes as follows:

All plane regular polygons have exterior angles summing to four right angles
All triangles [or squares, etc.] are plane regular polygons

Therefore, all triangles have exterior angles summing to four right angles

This is a scientific syllogism of form *AAA*-1 (*Barbara*), with " plane regular polygons " as the middle term (cause).

If you take the thing on which the cause [operates] only in part,
14 | then it [i.e., the cause] is the greater.[15]
He means that if you make the subject partial [with respect to the cause], then its cause will be greater than it, i.e., superior to it.
15 Then he gave | an explanatory example of this. He said:
An example of this is [the term] " the existence of [16] exterior angles equal to four right angles," which is greater [in applicability]
16 | than what pertains [solely] to the triangle and the square. But if you take all of them together [viz. all of the figures whose exterior angles amount to four right angles], then they [i.e., the two terms at issue] are equal [in extent of application].[17]
17 He means by this that every plane | regular polygonal figure—whatever figure it be: triangle, or square, or pentagon, or other
18 | regular polygonal figure—[is such that] if each of its sides is extended in one direction, then the sum of the exterior angles
19 | that result is equal to four right angles.
The demonstration of this is evident to anyone who has a little
20 knowledge | of geometry. This is so because the sum of the [interior] angles of a triangle is equal to two right angles, and the
21 [interior] angles of every [square] polygonal figure | are equal to four right angles, because it is divisible into two triangles. And
22 likewise every pentagon—since the sum of its angles | is equal to six right angles, whether or not the pentagon is irregular or
23 regular, because it is divisible into three triangles | and the angles of every triangle are equal to two right angles—will therefore have its sum [of interior angles] be six right angles. And likewise
ב ١ the hexagon has [interior angles] equal | to eight right angles. And in general, every regular polygonal figure increases its angles
2 upon the angles of the figure that | precedes it by two right angles.
If this is established, and we have a triangle, such as the triangle
3 *ABC*, or a square such as the square *DEFG*, | or a pentagon such as the pentagon *HIJKL*, and so on, and we extend each one of
4 their sides in this fashion [as illustrated], | then the exterior angles of the triangle will be equal to four right angles; and similarly the

---

[15] *Posterior Analytics*, 99a19. See 158b6–7 above.
[16] The *k-w-n* here is missing in line 158b7.
[17] *Posterior Analytics*, 99a19–21. See 158b7–8 above.

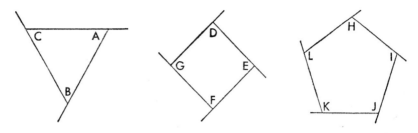

5 exterior angles | of the square will be equal to this measure, and similarly the [exterior] angles of the pentagon.

6 This is so because in the triangle *ABC* the interior angle | *A* and the exterior [angle] adjacent to it are equal to two right angles. And likewise the angle *B* and the one adjacent to it; and similarly

7 the angle | *C* and the one adjacent to it. Therefore the sum total of all six of the angles is equal to six right angles, from which one

8 is to drop the interior angles of [the triangle] *ABC*, | which are equal to two right angles, so that the remaining exterior angles are equal to four right angles. And similarly, it is shown in [the

9 case of] the square | *DEFG* that since every angle and the one adjacent to it is equal to two right angles, so that the sum-total of

10 the eight interior and exterior angles | is equal to eight right angles; dropping the interior angles, amounting to four right

11 angles, the exterior angles remain equal to | four right angles. And likewise in [the case of] the pentagon *HIJKL*, each [interior] angle and the exterior angle adjacent to it equals two right angles,

12 so that | the sum-total of them all is equal to ten right angles; dropping the interior angles, amounting to six right angles, the

13 exterior [angles] remain, equal to | four right angles. And similarly for the other [regular polygonal] figures.

It is possible to demonstrate this fact by a general discussion,

14 without | our following in it [i.e., the demonstration] the line of reasoning which we followed above. This general procedure is as follows:

15 The demonstration of this | is that the number of the exterior and interior angles of every regular polygonal figure, if each of its

16 sides is extended, | is equal to twice the number of the sides, because every pair of two angles is formed by each side; and the

17 interior | and the exterior [angles] [upon each side] are equal to
two right angles. However the number of sides [of the polygon]
is equal to the number of triangles into which it is divisible [from
18 its center] with | two of its sides. [Thus] the [total] number of
its triangles is half the number of right angles into which it is
19 divisible, because each | of its triangles has two right angles.
[Therefore] the number of interior and exterior angles of every
9b 1 [regular polygonal] figure is [equal to] the number of angles | of
the triangles into which each of the [regular polygonal] figures is
divisible. But the interior angles are [equal] in number to the
2 angles | of the triangles into which it [i.e., the polygon] is divisible,
except for the angles of two triangles,[18] so that the remaining
exterior angles are [equal] in number to the angles of two triangles.
3 But the angles of two triangles | are equal to four right angles, so
that the exterior angles of every [regular polygonal] figure are
4 equal to four right angles. | And this is what we wished to
establish.

Therefore, this has made clear the meaning of Aristotle's
5 statement | " The exterior angles [of a regular polygon] are equal
to four right angles." [19] He means this for every [polygonal]
6 figure with regular (i.e., equal) sides, as we have shown. | And
his statement " [This predicate] is greater [in applicability] than
what pertains [solely] to the triangle and the square " [20] is true,
without exaggeration, because it pertains to the pentagon also,
7 and the hexagon, and the entirety | of the figures with regular
(i.e., equal) sides; and therefore it extends beyond what pertains
[solely] to the triangle and the square. And his statement " But
8 if you take | all of them together, then they are all equal " [21]
means that if we put forward the [following] judgment and say
9 that " Every figure with regular (i.e., equal) sides, | has its
exterior angles equal to four right angles," then the judgment does

---

[18] Since the sum of all the center-based angles of all these triangles is 180°.
Observe that the sense of the discussion requires that we place " except for the
angles of two triangles " here instead of at the end of the preceding sentence; as
the manuscript does.
[19] Cf. 158b6–7 above.
[20] Cf. 158b7 above.
[21] Cf. 158b8 above.

not extend [in potential applicability] beyond what it judges
10 about, because | no [plane] figure other than one with regular
(i.e., equal) sides exists whose exterior angles are equal to four
11 | right angles.

As for his statement " And this is so in all things (i.e., figures) [22]
12 whose four exterior angles [23] are equal to | four right angles," [24]
this is an error of the translator's and must needs say the following:
13 " And this is so in all things (i.e., figures) | whose exterior angles
are equal to four right angles," without specifying in the statement
14 that the | exterior angles are four, because the exterior angles of
the pentagon are five [in number] and these are [also] equal to
15 four right angles | and the exterior angle of a hexagon are six and
16 these [too] are equal to four right angles, and likewise | with the
other [regular polygonal] figures, *ad infinitum*. No matter how
17 numerous the exterior angles may be, they will equal | four right
angles. It would make no sense if he [Aristotle] made the limita-
tion to four, but rather this is a gross error in the translation.
18 *The why.* | The master Abū ʿAlī ibn Sīnā mentioned this
example when he discoursed about *Posterior Analytics* in his book
19 | entitled *Al-Shifāʾ* and [also] in his book entitled *Al-Awsat
al-jurjānī.* [However], he made a mistake about it in both of these
20 books. | He made the example particular, since he wished to
21 oppose Aristotle's statement in *Posterior Analytics*— | in the section
regarding the matter in the first Book [25]—that the universal
22 demonstration is superior to the particular. In fact, | Aristotle
mentions this example in two places in this book; once in the first
23 Book, | in the chapter which we have just mentioned, [26] and again
160a 1 in the second Book, [27] in the place which we have cited | in
opposing the translation of Abū Bishr.

As to the master Abū ʿAlī ibn Sīnā, God rest his soul, he
2 discussed the example | regarding which we said that it is from

[22] Thus in the margin.
[23] The text again reads: " whose *four* exterior angles." But the *four* is
unwanted here, as the immediately following discussion rightly insists.
[24] Cf. 158b8–9 above.
[25] *Posterior Analytics*, I, iv.
[26] Namely *Posterior Analytics*, I, iv.
[27] *Posterior Analytics*, II, xvii.

the first Book [of *Posterior Analytics*]. But he made it particular,
3 and he dropped it from the second Book in favor of the first. | We
shall [now] report upon this section on the basis [28] of the discussion [29] of Avicenna in both of his books.

4 The master Abū ʿAlī ibn Sīnā said in | the chapter entitled
" On [the Thesis] that The Universal Affirmative Direct Demon-
5 stration is Superior to its Opposites " in the third Book | of the
fifth division of the *Scientia Prima* (*al-ḥikmat al-ūlā*) of the *Kitāb
al-shifāʾ* as follows:

6   The universal | is that which gives to the particular what it
(i.e., the particular) has essentially. The universal is the end
(i.e., terminus) of inquiry regarding " why? " Inquiry ends there
7 | where we say that we know a thing. For instance, if a questioner
asks " Why did so-and-so come? " and it is said " To take some
8 money," and he says, " Why did he take it? " and it is said | " To
settle an obligation with his creditor," and he says, " And why did
he settle? " and it is said " So as not to be unjust." Since the inquiry
9 for knowledge comes to an end in this case | and such examples, the
mind has come to rest at something it [really] knows. It is certain
that the inquiry for the *why?* in such examples comes to an end at
10 | something that cannot be gone beyond, and this is the most general
and highest matter which necessitates the judgment both for itself
11 and for other things it causes. | And this [highest reason] is the
required cause.

And similarly, if we ask regarding particulars, " Why are the
12 exterior angles of *this* triangle | equal to four right angles? " and if
we answered with something particular, saying " Because it is made
13 of gold " and " Because it is printed | on a robe " or " Because it is
this triangle " there would be nothing in these answers regarding the
14 essential cause which is now required. | [Rather] we [should] say,
" Because the triangle is enclosed by three straight lines, each of
which, if extended, forms about itself [two angles] equal to two right
15 angles; | and so the totality of them are six right angles, two of which
are interior, so that there remain four [right angles] for the exterior
16 ones." And so, | since in order to give the cause we had need for a
universal demonstration, it will not be possible for us to demonstrate
17 such a judgment about | [a triangle] with two equal sides in a
universal demonstration [about an arbitrary triangle], unless we
say it is the triangle the character of whose sides is such-and-such.

[28] Literally: *by the source.*
[29] Read *kalām* for *kalā.*

18 | He [Avicenna] also says in his book *Fī 'l-awsaṭ al-jurjānī*—in the first Book of the *Liber de demonstratione* [Kitāb al-burhān], in

19 | the chapter entitled " That universal demonstration is superior to the particular "—these words also, namely:

20 | ... because the causal syllogism must be universal, since its predicate is primary and essential. The universal completes the

21 cause in giving the predicate and its particular cause. | Here the last question regarding the *why?* comes to a stop. For example: If it is said " Why did so-and-so come? " and it is said [in reply] " To

22 take away some money," | and when it is said *why?*, it is said " To settle an obligation with his creditor," and when it is said *why?* it is said " So as not to be unjust," then this [last statement] will be

23 the stopping-point of the *why?* here, | and it is the universal judgment and the final cause.

Now if it is asked, " Why are triangles such that their exterior angles opposite . . . " [30]

C. The Arabic Text of Ibn al-Ṣalāḥ's Treatise

158b 1   استعنت بالله سبحانه   بسم الله الرحمن الرحيم

2
3 شرح فصل فى اخر المقاله الثانيه من كتاب ارسطوطاليس فى البرهان | واصلاح

4 خطأ فيه للشيخ ابى الفتوح احمد بن محمد بن السرى رحمه الله. | قال ارسطوطاليس فى اخر المقاله الثانيه من كتابه فى البرهان بنقــل ابى بشر

5 متى بن | يونس القنانى. فاما فى العله والامر الذى العله علته والامر الذى العله

6 له هى لازمه بعضها | بعضا فالحال فيه هذه الحال وهى انك ان انت اخذت

7 الشىء الذى العله علته فى الجزئيه فهو | اكثر مثال ذلك كون [31] الزوايا

8 الخارجه مساويه لاربع قوايم هى ازيد مما للمثلث والمربع فاما | اذا اخذت جميعها فهى بالتساوى وذلك ان جميع الاشياء [32] التى زواياها الاربع الخارجه

9 مساويه لاربع زوايا قايمه فالاوسط على مثال واحد تفسير ذلك يعنى ان

10 العله وهو | الحد الاوسط فى القياس والمعلول وهو الذى سماه الامر الذى

---

[30] The last word of this line is illegible. And with this line, the Istanbul manuscript of our treatise comes to an end.

[31] The MS does not give the word كون, but see line 158b15.

[32] In the margin: يعنى الاشكال.

64

11 العله له وهو الحد المحمول | فى القياس والموضوع وهو الحد الموضوع فى

12 القياس وهو الذى سهاه الامر الذى | العله علته ثلاثتها متلازمه لا يفضل

13 بعضها على بعض لكن ان نحن اخذنا بعض انواع الموضوع | فضلت العله

عليه وذلك معنى قوله ان انت اخذت الشىء الذى العله علته فى الجزئيه

14 | فهو اكثر يعنى ان انت جعلت الموضوع جزئيا فالعله تكون اكثر منه اى

15 تفضل عليه. ثم ضرب | لذلك مثالا تعليميا فقال مثال ذلك كون الزوايا

16 الخارجه مساويه لاربع قوايم هى ازيد | مما للمثلث والمربع فاما اذا اخذت

17 جميعها فهى بالتساوى. يعنى بذلك ان كل شكل مسطح | مستقيم الاضلاع

اى شكل كان مثلثا كان او مربعا او مخمسا او غير ذلك من الاشكال

18 | المستقيمه الاضلاع اذا اخرج كل واحد من اضلاعه فى جهه واحده فان

19 مجموع الزوايا | الخارجه التى تحدث تساوى اربع قوايم وبرهان ذلك ظاهر

20 لمن كان عنده ادنى علم | من الهندسه وذلك انه قد بان ان زوايا المثلث تساوى

21 قايمتين وزوايا كل شكل ذى | اضلاع تساوى اربع قوايم لانه ينقسم الى

22 مثلثين وكذلك كل مخمس فان مجموع زواياه | تساوى ست قوايم كيف

كان المخمس مختلف الاضلاع او متساويا لانه ينقسم الى ثلث مثالث

23 | وكل مثلث فزواياه تساوى قايمتين فيكون مجموعها ست قوايم وكذلك المسدس

1 159a تساوى || زواياه ثمان قوايم وبالجمله كل شكل مستقيم الاضلاع تزيد زواياه

2 على زوايا الشكل الذى | قبله بزاويتين قايمتين فاذ اثبت هذا وكان لنا مثلث

3 كمثلث (ابج) ومربع كمربع (دهرح) | ومخمس كمخمس (طكلمن) او

4 غير ذلك واخرجنا كل واحد من اضلاعها على هذه الصوره | كانت زوايا

5 المثلث الخارجه تساوى اربع قوايم وكذلك زوايا | المربع الخارجه تساوى

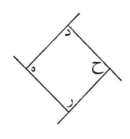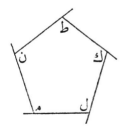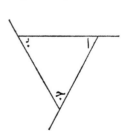

6 هذا المقدار وكذلك زوايا المخمس وذلك ان فى مثلث (ابج) زاويه | (ا) الداخله
والتى تليها الخارجه تساوى قايمتين وكذلك زاويه (ب) والتى تليها وكذلك
7 زاويه | (ج) والتى تليها فمجموع الست زوايا تساوى ست زوايا قايمه تسقط
8 منها زوايا (ابج) الداخله | وهى تساوى قايمتين فتبقى الزوايا الخارجه تساوى
9 اربع زوايا قايمه وكذلك يتبين فى مربع | (دهرح) ان كل زاويه وما تليها
10 تساوى قايمتين فيكون مجموع الثمان الزوايا الداخله والخارجه | تساوى ثمان
زوايا قايمه تسقط الزوايا الداخله باربع قوايم تبقى الزوايا الخارجه تساوى
11 | اربع قوايم وكذلك فى مخمس (طكلمن) كل زاويه وما تليها من الخارجه
12 تساوى قايمتين فيكون | مجموعها كلها تساوى عشر قوايم تسقط الداخله
13 بست قوايم تبقى الخارجه تساوى | اربع قوايم وكذلك فى غير ذلك من
14 الاشكال وقد يمكن ان نبرهن هذا المعنى بكلام كلى من | غير ان نسلك
فيه سبيل الاستقراء الذى سلكناه قبل والطريق الكلى هو هذا. برهان ذلك
15 | ان عدد الزوايا الخارجه والداخله من كل شكل مستقيم الاضلاع اذا اخرج
16 كل واحد من | اضلاعه تساوى ضعف عدد اضلاعه لان كل زاويتين عن
17 ضبتى ضلع من اضلاعه الداخله | والخارجه تساوى قايمتين لكن عدد
18 اضلاعه تساوى عده المثلثات التى ينقسم اليها اى | ضلعين من اضلاعه
19 وعده المثلثات نصف عده الزوايا القايمه التى ينقسم اليها لان كل | مثلث
له زاويتان قايمتان تكون عده الزوايا الداخله والخارجه من كل شكل بعده
15؟ زوايا || المثلثات التى انقسم اليها كل شكل سوى زوايا مثلثين لكن الزوايا
2 الداخله بعدد زوايا | المثلثات التى انقسم اليها فتبقى الزوايا الخارجه بعدد زوايا
3 مثلثين لكن زوايا مثلثين | تساوى اربع زوايا قايمه فاذا الزوايه الخارجه من
4 كل شكل تساوى اربع زوايا | قايمه وذلك ما اردنا ان نبين. فقد بان من
5 ذلك معنى قول ارسطوطاليس | الزوايه الخارجه مساويه لاربع زوايا قايمه
6 يعنى لكل شكل مستقيم الخطوط كما بينا | وقوله ازيد مما للمثلث والمربع صحيح
7 لا مزيد فيه لانها للمخمس ايضا وللمسدس ولجميع | الاشكال المستقيمه
8 الخطوط فهى تفضل على المثلث والمربع. وقوله فاما اذا اخذت | جميعها

66

فهى متساويه يعنى اذا نحن اطلقنا الحكم وقلنا ان كل شكل مستقيم الخطوط

9 فان | زواياه الخارجه تساوى اربع زوايا قايمه كان الحكم لا يفضل على

10 المحكوم عليه لانه | لا يوجد من غير الاشكال المستقيمه الخطوط شكل تساوى

11 زواياه الخارجه لاربع | قوايم. واما قوله ان جميع الاشياء³³ التى زواياها

12 الاربع الخارجه مساويه | لاربع زوايا قايمه فهو خطأ من المترجم وينبغى

13 ان يقال هكذا. وذلك ان جميع الاشياء | التى زواياها الخارجه مساويه لاربع

14 زوايا قايمه من غير ان يخصص بقوله زواياها | الاربع الخارجه لان الزوايا

15 الخارجه من المخمس هى خمس وهى تساوى اربع زوايا | قايمه والزوايا الخارجه من المسدس هى ست وهى تساوى اربع زوايا قايمه وكذلك

16 | غير ذلك من الاشكال الغير المتناهيه مها كثرت الزوايا الخارجه كم كانت

17 فهى تساوى | اربع زوايا قايمه فلا معنى اذا لتخصيصه بالاربع وهو خطأ

18 فى الترجمه فاحش. واللم. | وذكر الرئيس ابو على بن سينا هذا المثال حيث

19 تكلم فى كتاب البرهان فى كتابه | الموسوم بالشفاء وفى كتابه الموسوم بالاوسط

20 الجرجانى واخطأ فيه فى كلى الكتابين | جعل المثال جزئيا وذلك حيث اراد

21 ان يحادى كلام ارسطوطاليس فى كتاب البرهان | فى الفصل الذى يتكلم فيه فى المقاله الاولى فى ان البرهان الكلى افضل من الجزئى وذلك ان

22 | ارسطوطاليس ذكر هذا المثال فى موضعين من هذا الكتاب احدهما فى المقاله

23 الاولى | فى الفصل الذى ذكرناه الان والاخر فى المقاله الثانيه فى الموضع الذى حكيناه || حديا فى نقل ابى بشر واما الرئيس ابو على بن سينا رحمه الله

160a 1

2 فانه ذكر المثال فى | الذى ذكرنا من المقاله الاولى وجعله جزئيا واسقطه من

3 المقاله الثانيه بالواحده | ونحن نحكى الفصل بنص كلا[م] بن سينا فى كلى

4 الكتابين. قال الرئيس ابو على بن سينا فى | الفصل الذى عنوانه فى ان البرهان

5 الكلى والموجب والمستقيم افضل من مقابله فى المقاله | الثالثه من الفن الخامس

6 من الحكمه الاولى من كتاب الشفاء هذا الكلام. فالكلى هو | الذى يعطى الجزئى ما له بذاته والكلى هو الذى عنده نهايه البحث عن لم وعند تناهى

---

³³ In the margin: يعنى الاشكال.

67

7 البحث | ما نظن انا علمنا الشىء كما لو سأل سايل لم جاء فلان فقيل

8 ليأخذ مالا فقال لم يأخذ قيل | ليقضى دين غريمه قيل ولم يقضى قيل لكى

9 لا يكون ظالما فاذا وقف البحث عن اللم عند هذا | وامثاله فقد سكنت

10 النفس الى معلومها ولا محاله ان بحث اللم فى امثال هذا ينتهى الى | امر لا

يتجاوز عنه ويكون هو الامر الاعم الاعلى الذى يلزمه الحكم لنفسه ولغيره

11 سببه | وهو العله المطلوبه وكذلك ان سئلنا عن الجزئيات ان هذا المثلث لم

12 زواياه الخارجه | مساويه لاربع زوايا قوايم واجبنا بشىء جزئى فقلنا لانـه من ذهب

13 و لانـه مخطوط | فى ثوب او لانه هذا المثلث لم يكن شىء من هذا جوابا عن

14 العله الذاتيه التى تطلب الان | نقول لانه شكل يحيط به ثلث خطوط مستقيمه

15 كل واحد اذا اخرج ارتسم حوله مساويتان | لقايمتين فيكون جميعها ست زوايا

16 قايمه اثنتان منها داخلتان فبقى الخارج اربعا فنحن | اذا فى اعطاء العله

نضطر الى البرهان على الكلى وليس ممكنا ان نبرهن عـلى هـذا الحـكم فى

17 | المتساوى الساقين برهانا كليا الا ان نقول انه مثلث حال اضلاعه كذا

18 وكذا. | وقال ايضا فى كتابه فى الاوسط الجرجانى فى المقاله الاولى من كتاب

19 البرهان فى | الفصل الذى عنوانه فى ان البرهان الكلى افضل مـن الجـزئى هذا

20 الكلام ايضا وهو | ولان قياس العله انها تكون للكلى لان الحمل له اولى

21 وبذاته ثم الكلى علته فى اعطاء الحمل وعلته | الجزئى وهناك يقف اخر السؤال

22 عن اللم مثلا. اذا قيل لم جاء فلان فقيل ليأخذ مالا | فان قيل لم قيل ليقضى

23 دين غريمه فان قيل لم قيل لكى لا يكون ظالما فيكون وقوف اللم هنا | وهو

الحكم الكلى والعله الاخيره. وان قيل لم كان المثلث زواياه الخارجه معاداه ( )[34]

---

[34] Illegible word of 3-4 letters.

VI

THE CONCEPT OF EXISTENCE IN ARABIC LOGIC AND PHILOSOPHY

1. Introduction

The concept of existence has received a great deal of attention from philosophers and logicians in recent years. These studies proceeded in complete unawareness that some of the distinctions drawn and ideas adduced were anticipated in discussions by Arabic philosophers of the 9th and 13th centuries which resulted from an extensive preoccupation with the concept of existence. The purpose of the present chapter is to call attention to—and to describe certain interesting features of—these older treatments of currently relevant themes. The reader can be assured of surprises if he thinks that the idea of " intentional inexistence " was born in the school of F. Brentano, that the denial that *existence* is a predicate was an invention of Kant's, or that B. Russell originated the teaching that the truth of a singular subject-predicate statement required the existence of its subject.

2. The Mu'tazilite Schools of Baghdad and Basra (9th Century)

In the 9th century, the Mu'tazilites (Muslim scholastic theologians) separated into two schools, one centered at Baghdad and the other at Basra.[1] Both of these schools occupied themselves extensively with the question: What is a thing (*shay'*)? Certain scholars

---

[1] The ensuing account is taken primarily from: H. S. Nyberg, art. " al-Mu'tazila " in *Handwörterbuch des Islam* (ed. A. J. Wensinck and J. H. Kramers [Leiden, 1941]), pp. 556–562; English version in *Shorter Encyclopedia of Islam*

defined this—following the Stoics, as we shall see—as *anything whose concept can be known and of which something could be said.*[2] Existence (*wujūd*) does not matter: it is only an attribute or quality which, like other qualities, a thing may or may not possess. With it, the thing becomes an entity or existent (*mawjūd*); without it a nonentity or nonexistent (*ma'dūm*). Nonexistents have a mode of subsistence (*thubūt*) of their own, and come with the full equipment of substance and accident, genus and species: the realism of the Mu'tazilite realm of nonexistence is reminiscent of Plato's realm of the Ideas.[3]

In their concern with the question: *What is a thing?* the Mu'tazilites divided into sub-schools. One influential group taught that there are four kinds of things: existents (entities), nonexistents (nonentities), states, and relationships.[4] States and relationships—and the qualities of things generally—were thought to correspond to a status intermediate between that of an existent and of a nonexistent.[5]

(ed. H. A. R. Gibb and J. H. Kramers [Leiden, 1953]), pp. 421-427. D. B. MacDonald, *The Development of Muslim Theology, Jurisprudence, and Constitutional Theory* (London, 1903; reprinted, Lahore, 1960), pp. 159–160 of the reprint. (MacDonald's presentation closely follows that of Heinrich Steiner, *Die Mu'taziliten* [Leipzig, 1865], pp. 80–85.) A. N. Nader, *Le système philosophique des Mu'tazila* (Beirut, 1956) [see especially ch. I of pt. II]. The principal primary source is al-Shahrastānī's *Kitāb al-milal wa-'l-niḥal* (" Book of Religious and Philosophical Sects "), ed. W. Cureton (2 vols., London, 1842, 1846) and tr. into German by T. Haarbrücker (2 vols., Halle, 1850, 1851); see pp. 79–88 of vol. I of Haarbrücker's translation. Cf. also A. Biram (ed.): Al-Naisābūrī, *Die atomistische Substanzlehre aus dem Buch der Streitfragen zwischen Basrensern und Baghdadensern* (Leiden, 1902). The single most comprehensive treatment of the relevant issues is Otto Pretzl, " Die frühislamische Attributenlehre," published in the *Sitzungsberichte der Bayerischen Akademie der Wissenschaften*, Philosophisch-historische Abteilung (München, 1940); 63 pp.

[2] This definition of *shay'* was not, strictly speaking, original with the theologians in Islam, but was taken by them from the Arab grammarians and lexicographers to support their views. Cf. H. Ritter (ed.), *Die dogmatischen Lehren der Anhänger des Islam von Abu l-Hasan 'Alī ibn Ismā'īl al-Ash'arī* (Istanbul, 1929; *Bibliotheca Islamica* I; 2d edition, Wiesbaden, 1963), pp. 36 ff., 42, 44–45, 55, 70, 158–162. See also al-Jurjānī, *Kitāb al-ta'rīfāt,* s.v.; *Taṭ al-'arūs,* s.v.; and E. W. Lane, *Arabic and English Lexicon,* pt. 4, p. 1626a.

[3] See Nader, *op. cit.,* pp. 140–141.

[4] The views presented here are in the main those of one of the later Mu'tazilites, Abū Hāshim (d. 933), who attempted to reconcile the theories of his father, al-Jubbā'ī (d. 915), with Islamic orthodoxy by declaring God's attributes to be " states " (*ḥāl;* pl., *aḥwāl*). It is not here our aim to examine the various teachings of different sects of Mu'tazilites on these matters. The reader can find some information on the matter in H. S. Nyberg's article cited in footnote 1 above.

[5] Abū Hāshim ibn al-Jubbā'ī of Basra (d. 933)—and other Mu'tazilites—held that states and relationships are purely subjective to the mind of the perceiver,

This Muʻtazilite theory of nonexistence (*al-ʻadam*) and of modes of being intermediate between existence and nonexistence had a special bearing upon the doctrine of creation. God added but the single quality of existence and things which but for this would have remained nonentities became realized as actual. Here, then, we have a version of a doctrine of preexistent substances. The Muslim theologians used the concept of nonentities to explain God's knowledge of the nonexistent possible world before its actual existence.[6] The awkward theological consequence of setting up a realm of nonexistents which has quasi-being but is uncreated and co-eternal with the deity was got over by putting this realm into the mind of God—an anticipation of Leibniz' solution to the same problem.

3. AL-FĀRĀBĪ (CA. 873–950) [7]

In al-Fārābī we find a denial that existence is a quality. He wrote (evidently in opposition to the Muʻtazilite teaching that existence is an attribute):

Question: Does the proposition " Man exists " have a predicate or not?

Answer: This is a problem on which both the ancients and the moderns disagree; some say that this sentence has no predicate, and some say that it has a predicate. To my mind, both of these judgments are in a way correct, each in its own way. This is so because when a *natural scientist* who investigates perishable things considers this sentence

existing or rather subsisting—in the manner of nonexistents—mentally but not objectively. On the basis of such a qualified realism, states and relationships were put into an ontological category intermediate between that of existents and nonexistents. See T. J. de Boer, *The History of Philosophy in Islam* (tr. E. R. Jones; London, 1903; reprinted 1961), p. 55. Muʻammar (fl. ca. 900) became widely noted in Islam because he not only accepted relations, but taught that there were infinitely many of them. (See S. van den Bergh, *Averroes' Tahāfut al-Tahāfut*, vol. II [Notes; London, 1954], p. 60 [n. 81.2].) In getting qualities out of the domain of the existent, the Islamic theologians circumvented the problem posed for the strict unity of God by the plurality of His attributes.

[6] Van den Bergh, *op. cit.*, pp. 4–5 (n. 3.6). On the medieval Latin reaction to one aspect of the Arabic views on subsistence-in-the-mind see A. Maurer, " *Ens diminutum*: a Note on its Origin and Meaning," *Mediaeval Studies*, vol. 12 (1950), pp. 216–222.

[7] Bio-bibliographical information regarding all the Arabic logicians to be discussed can be found in N. Rescher, *The Development of Arabic Logic* (Pittsburgh, 1964). For al-Fārābī specifically see N. Rescher, *Al-Fārābī: An Annotated Bibliography* (Pittsburgh, 1962).

F

(and similar ones) it has no predicate, for the existence of a thing is nothing other than the thing itself, and [for the scientist] a predicate must furnish information about what exists and what is excluded from being.[8] Regarded from this point of view, this proposition does not have a predicate. But when a *logician* investigates this proposition, he will treat it as composed of two expressions, each forming part of it, and it [i.e., the composite proposition] is liable to truth and falsehood. And so it does have a predicate from this point of view. Therefore the assertions are both together correct, but each of them only in a certain way.[9]

Grammatically, " Man exists " is a complete sentence, with a grammatical subject, " man," and a grammatical predicate, " exists." Thus due to close parallelism between the logical and the grammatical relations (especially in Arabic) al-Fārābī unhesitatingly classes " exists " as a legitimate grammatical (or logical) predicate. Even Kant agrees with this, affirming that: " *zum logischen Prädicate kann alles dienen, was man will.*" Consideration of the question " Is ' exists ' a predicate? " and of the logical issues involved in it thus goes back at least to the 9th century. Further, al-Fārābī's insistence that the attribution of existence to an object adds nothing to its characterization, and provides no new information about it, effectively anticipates Kant's thesis that: " *Sein ist offenbar kein reales Prädicat, d. i. ein Begriff von irgend etwas, was zum Begriffe eines Dinges hinzukommen könne.*"

4. AVICENNA (980–1037)

In Avicenna's treatise *Dānesh-nāme* he argued:

The difference between the two propositions [" Zayd is a being-that-does-not-see " and " Zayd is not a being-that-sees "] is this, that if Zayd

---

[8] That is to say the predicate must give information regarding the nature (*māhīya*, " what "-ness, *quidditas*) of the thing in question. The existence of a thing (its *huwīya*, " that "-ness, *esse*) is not a part of its essence.

[9] *Alfārābī's Philosophische Abhandlungen*, ed. by F. Dieterici (Leiden, 1890), p. 90. For further discussion of this text see the writer's *Studies in the History of Arabic Logic* (Pittsburgh, 1963), pp. 39–42. " Everything possible in itself is, when its being is educed into act, forthwith necessary through another. For, it cannot but be that actual existence either be or not be its true predicate. But it is contradictory that actual existence be not its true predicate, else it would be impossible. It remains, therefore, that actual existence is its true predicate. But, then, either its being is necessary or not necessary. . . . " *Avicennae: Metaphysices Compendium*, ed. N. Carame (Romae, Pont. Institut. Orientalium Studiorum, 1926), Cap. iii, pp. 69–70. Cited in the English translation by Gerard Smith, " Avicenna and the Possibles," *The New Scholasticism*, vol. 17 (1943), p. 342.

does not exist in the world, you can say " Zayd is not a being-that-sees," because this Zayd who does not exist is not a being-that-sees; but it is not correct to say " Zayd is a being-that-does-not-see " so long as Zayd does not exist.[10]

Avicenna is thus committed to the thesis that if ϕ is a genuine predicate, then

$$\frac{\text{``}\phi a\text{'' is true}}{\text{E}!a}$$

is a valid inference, (" E!a " being construed as stating that a exists). And correspondingly an important difference must be drawn between the assignment of a negation-predicate and the negation of a predicate assignment: [11]

$$[\sim \phi]a \rightarrow \text{E}!a$$
$$\sim [\phi a] \leftrightarrow (\sim \text{E}!a \text{ v } [\sim \phi]a)$$

The proposition " Zayd is a being-that-does-not-see " is an affirmative one, as Avicenna rightly insists, and he lays it down that such a proposition is never true of a singular subject that does not exist.[12]

This doctrine that only actual existents can bear predicates obviously has the significant consequence in that it pretty well rules out the very conception of nonexistents. If it is never true that they have a certain property, they will not have qualities and cannot even be characterized or defined.

---

[10] M. Achena and H. Massé (tr's), *Avicenne; Le Livre de Science*, vol. I (Paris, 1955), p. 38. Zayd is the paradigm individual for the Arab logicians—like Plato or Socrates for the Latin medievals.

[11] See A. M. Goichon (tr.), *Ibn Sīnā: Livre de Directives et Remarques* (Paris, 1951), pp. 125–126, where this point is developed. The position at issue here, as well as the thesis that there is no true predication save of existents, go back to Aristotle's discussion in *Categories* x, 13b12–19, where, however, the issue is beclouded by talk of contrary rather than contradictory predications.

[12] *Ibid.*, pp. 37–38. " Everything possible in itself is, when its being is educed into act, forthwith necessary through another. For, it cannot but be that actual existence either be or not be its true predicate. But it is contradictory that actual existence be not its true predicate, else it would be impossible. It remains, therefore, that actual existence is its true predicate. But, then, either its being is necessary or not necessary. . . . " *Avicennae: Metaphysics Compendium*, ed. N. Carame (Romae, Pont. Institut. Orientalium Studiorum, 1926), cap. iii, pp. 69–70. Cited in the English translation by Gerard Smith, " Avicenna and the Posssibles," *The New Scholasticism*, vol. 17 (1943), p. 342.

5. Averroes (1126–1198)

With regard to the question of whether the world was *possibly* existent prior to its actual existence, Averroes maintained the negative. In line with the Aristotelian thesis that possibility presupposes actuality, Averroes maintained that the possibility of a world " demands an existing matter." [13] Arguing against al-Ghazālī's argument that if possibility requires an existent as its *locus essendi* then so does impossibility, and this consequence is absurd, Averroes meets the argument head-on:

> For impossibility is the negation of possibility, and, if possibility needs a substratum, impossibility which is the negation of this possibility requires a substratum too.[14]

The reasoning is that no judgment is true unless it states what is the case, and nothing can be the case unless it is about something: " All true intellectual concepts need a thing outside the soul; for truth, as it has been defined, is the agreement of what is in the soul with what is outside the soul." [15] This position of course requires a liberalized conception of something—as Aristotle insists *Metaphysics* Γ ii, 1003b10—even absolute privation or non-being is " something," namely the nonexistent.[16] We are brought back to the (Stoic) view that even " nothing " stands for something—although the " something " it stands for does not exist.[17]

The " substratum " at issue in Averroes' discussion is thus not strictly speaking a material one at all in the case of nonexistents, but immaterial, or rather, conceptual. We are, in effect, brought back to the dualistic ontology of existents and nonexistents.

The Averroist position differs, however, from that of Avicenna in

[13] S. van den Bergh (tr.), *Averroes' Tahāfut al-Tahāfut*, vol. I (London, 1954), p. 60; see also the translator's note *ad loc.* in vol. II (*op. cit.*), p. 46, and cf. p. 136 (n. 236.3).

[14] *Ibid.*, pp. 60–61.

[15] This definition follows that of Aristotle, *De Interp.*, ix, 19a33.

[16] Cf. van den Bergh, *op. cit.*, vol. II, p. 47 (nn. 61.6 and 61.7). Note, however, that Aristotle holds that the actual existence of something is not a requisite for its being thought about so that " Homer is a poet " does not entail " Homer *is* (*simpliciter*) [i.e., exists]." See *De interpretatione* xii, 21a23–28.

[17] Al-Ghazālī took the harder line, holding that, since the nonexistent does not exist, " nonexistence " does not mean anything and stands for nothing. (Van den Bergh, *op. cit.*, vol. II, p. 52 [n. 67.1].)

an interesting and important way. To exhibit this difference simply and clearly let us introduce two modes of " existential " indicators, E! for strictly *actual* existence and ∃! for all *possible* existence (applying alike to both existents and nonexistents). Then in Avicenna we have it that whenever ϕ is a genuine predicate (i.e., one whose application imputes the possession of a genuine quality) then

$$\frac{``\phi a" \text{ is true}}{E! a}$$

is a valid inference, so that " the possession of a quality requires the existence of the object." In Averroes, on the other hand, we have merely the weaker thesis that the inference

$$\frac{``\phi a" \text{ is true}}{\exists! a}$$

is valid, so that " no (predicative) judgment is true unless there is something of which it is true." The entities in question may, however, be not strictly *real* but merely *conceptual* existents.[18]

Like al-Fārābī before him, Averroes attacks the Muʿtazilite position that existence is an attribute (and that " exists " is a genuine predicate), and he attacks both al-Ghazālī and Avicenna on this point.[19] He maintains that " existence " has two senses, applying to (1) that which is actual (i.e., true), and (2) that which belongs to the supreme genus of all entities.[20] The first applies when we speak of " what is " in the sense of *what is the case*: thus " x exists " when x is a fact or state of affairs means " x is actually the case." [21] The second meaning applies when we say, for example, " Zayd exists "—existence here represents simply the genus of all actual things. In either case, Averroes insists:

> when we say that a thing exists, the word " exists " does not indicate an entity added to its essence outside the soul, which is the case when we say of a thing [for example] that it is white. It is here that Avicenna erred, for he believed that unity is an addition to the essence and also

[18] Cf. van den Bergh, *op. cit.*, vol. II, p. 70 (n. 118.1).
[19] Van den Bergh, *op. cit.*, vol. I, pp. 117–119 and 236; cf. the notes in vol. II, pp. 79–81 and 137 (n. 237.4).
[20] *Ibid.*, p. 179.
[21] See also *ibid.*, vol. II, pp. 4–5 (n. 3.6) where van den Bergh properly stresses that " thing " for Averroes comprises also " fact " and " event."

that existence, when we say that a thing exists, is an addition to the thing.[22]

Averroes' position accords with the contention urged by al-Fārābī against the Mu'tazilites: the *existence* of an existing thing is not to be taken as one of its qualities.

6. AL-QAZWĪNĪ AL-KĀTIBĪ (CA. 1220–1292?)

In the *Risālah al-Shamsiyyah* of al-Qazwīnī al-Kātibī [23] we find a discussion which largely follows that of Avicenna but with certain interesting twists. This author terms " *a* is non-φ " an *affirmative privative proposition* and the corresponding " *a* is not φ " an *indivisible negative proposition*. It is maintained that:

> The indivisible negative proposition . . . is more general (contains more) than the affirmative with privative predicate . . ., for the negation [i.e., the indivisible negative] may be true though the subject is a nonentity . . ., but the affirmation cannot be true [in such a case]: because affirmation is admissible only in regard to a thing of ascertained (or acknowledged) existence. . . . If the subject does exist the indivisible negative and affirmative privative propositions are equivalent.[24]

Like Avicenna, al-Qazwīnī al-Kātibī accepts the principle that a statement making an affirmative predication of a nonexistent cannot be true. His example of a nonentity is *the partner of God*. We cannot admit the truth of a predication to a nonentity for an affirmation cannot be true of it—" if we say that the partner of God is non-omnipotent, we admit that there is a partner." The negative proposition however can be true—" though there is no such thing as a partner of God, we can still say that if there were one he could not

---

[22] *Ibid.*, vol. I, p. 118. Averroes makes the interesting assertion that: " the term ' existent ' is attributed essentially to God and analogically to all other things in the way in which warmth is attributed [essentially] to fire and [analogically] to all warm things." (*Ibid.*, p. 179.)

[23] Aloys Sprenger (ed.), *Dictionary of the Technical Terms used in the Sciences of the Musulmans*, pt. II (Calcutta, 1862). Appendix I entitled " The Logic of the Arabians " gives a text edition of this work, together with a (somewhat incomplete) English translation. The omitted sections—which deal with modal logic—are translated in N. Rescher, *Temporal Modalities in Arabic Logic* (Dordrecht, 1967; Supplementary Series for *Foundations of Language*, Vol. 2).

[24] *Op. cit.*, p. 18 (§ 47).

be omnipotent." [25]   The governing principle is that if a does not exist, then

a is a ϕ

must be false, and

a is not a ϕ

must be true, regardless of the property represented by the predicate ϕ. (This principle agrees exactly with Russell's theory of descriptions whenever ' a ' represents a vacuous definite description.)

7. MODERN PERSPECTIVES

The conception of nonexistents has played an extensive role in modern times in the philosophy of the school of Franz Brentano, figuring in the notion of " intentional inexistence " developed in this school—especially in the theory of " objects " of Brentano's pupil Alexius Meinong.[26]   Nonexistent possibles were assigned an important place in logical theory by Hugh MacColl,[27] and Russell's " theory of descriptions " was designed to deal with the problem in a way inspired primarily by the semantical theory of Gottlob Frege. The logical machinery of " nondesignating singular terms " has been developed extensively in the past decade.[28]

The thesis—supported in somewhat different forms by both Avicenna and Averroes—that one can make the inferential step from

" ϕa " is true

to

a exists

[25] *Loc. cit.*

[26] For an account in English see J. N. Findlay, *Meinong's Theory of Objects and Values* (London, 1963; 2nd ed.).

[27] He published a long series of articles in *Mind* (1880–1906), which were ultimately incorporated into his *Symbolic Logic and Its Applications* (1906). MacColl's views—which for a time succumbed to the (generally misguided) criticisms of Bertrand Russell—are only now beginning to be recognized for their genuine importance. A brief sketch of MacColl's theory is given in the writer's paper cited in the next footnote. By way of contrast the reader may consult A. N. Prior's interesting paper " Nonentities " in R. J. Butler (ed.), *Analytical Philosophy* (London, 1962), pp. 120–132.

[28] N. Rescher, " On the Logic of Existence and Denotation," *The Philosophical Review*, vol. 68 (1959), pp. 157–180; T. Hailperin and H. Leblanc, " Non-Designating Singular Terms," *The Philosophical Review*, vol. 68 (1959), pp. 239–243; J. Hintikka, " Existential Presupposition and Existential Commitments," *The Journal of Philosophy*, vol. 56 (1959), pp. 125–137; J. Hintikka, " Towards a Theory of Definite Descriptions," *Analysis*, vol. 19 (1959), pp. 79–85; T. Smiley, " Sense Without Denotation," *Analysis*, vol. 20 (1960), pp. 125–135.

has been espoused by several logicians in recent years. Thus P. F. Strawson has propounded a sense of " subject-predicate statement " and that the question of the truth or falsity of a statement of this sort of the form " ϕa " would be said " not to arise " unless a actually existed.[29] Along the same lines, R. Harré [30] has argued that if " ϕa " has any truth-value at all (true or false), then it must be the case that $(\exists x)(x = a)$. The theory (which we have found to play a prominent role in Arabic logic) that " there is no predication save of existents " is very definitely a living doctrine in the logic of today.

8. Appendix: Stoic Origins

The Mu'tazilite elaboration of the doctrine of nonentities—and thus the entire course of Arabic discussions of the issue—derives from Stoic sources.[31] Its whole machinery of existents and nonexistents, and qualities, states, and relations goes back to this origin. We may be sure of this salient fact even though we cannot trace the exact course of transmission of ideas with all the desirable detail.[32] All the pieces of the intricate chess-game the Arabic philosophers played with the conception of existence were taken from the Stoics, even if some of the moves were original.

The Stoic theory of categories is summarized in Mates' monograph as follows:

> Compared with Aristotle's ten categories, those of the Stoics number only four, plus one " highest notion." The highest notion was called *to ti*, " the indefinite something," and the four categories were:

[29] *Introduction to Logical Theory* (London, 1952), ch. vi.
[30] " A Note on Existence Propositions," *The Philosophical Review*, vol. 65 (1956), pp. 548–549. Cf. the writer's review of this paper in *The Journal of Symbolic Logic*, vol. 21 (1956), p. 384.
[31] Van den Bergh, *op. cit.*; Von Arnim, *Stoicorum Veterorum Fragmenta*; vol. II, pp. 48–49, 118–122, 131–133; E. Bréhier, *La Théorie des incorporels dans l'ancien Stoicisme* (2e ed., Paris, 1928). This Stoic provenience is recognized by van den Bergh only in part, and by Nader (*op. cit.*, pp. 143–144) not at all. (Nader [pp. 143–144] traces the Mu'tazilite doctrine back directly to the Aristotelian teaching that all being requires a preexistent possibility which must in turn have a foothold in some manner of actual existence.)
[32] See S. Horowitz, " Ueber den Einfluss des Stoicismus auf die Entwicklung der Philosophie bei den Arabern," *Zeitschrift der deutschen morgenländischen Gesellschaft*, vol. 57 (1903), pp. 177 ff.; and *idem*, " Ueber den Einfluss der griechischen Philosophie auf die Entwicklung des Kalām " (Breslau, 1909; Jahresbericht des jüdisch-theologischen Seminars zu Breslau). But see also Giuseppe Furlani, " Sur le stoicisme de Bardesane d'Edesse," *Archiv Orientálni*, vol. 9 (Prague, 1937), pp. 347–352.

(1) *to hypokeimenon*   subject or substratum
(2) *to poion*   quality
(3) *to pōs echon*   state
(4) *to pros ti pōs echon* relation

We are told that these four categories are so related to one another that every preceding category is contained in and more accurately determined by the next succeeding one.[33]

The Arabic term *shay'* (thing)—defined by the theologians as *huwa mā yajūz an yukhbara 'anhu* (" that which it is possible to speak [or: ' predicate '] about ") [34] corresponds to the Stoic *ti* (" something ") which applies to whatever can be meant, the false and the nonexistent included [35]—whatever can be represented by a *lekton* (meaningful expression).

Within the domain of the *ti* (or entity in the very widest sense) lies the *hypokeimenon* (Arabic: *mawjūd*) or actually extant substance.

The Stoic *to poion* or *poiotēs* (" quality ") corresponds to the Arabic *kayfiyyah*. The Stoic thesis of successive containment is clearly the basis for the doctrine that only actual existents can possess qualities.[36] (This doctrine is apparently the ultimate foundation for the contention of al-Fārābī—and certain ancients?—that existence is not a quality and " exists " not a predicate.)

---

[33] Benson Mates, *Stoic Logic* (Berkeley and Los Angeles, 1961; originally published as vol. 26 of the University of California Publications in Philosophy). Mates here follows the more extensive discussion of E. Zeller, *Die Philosophie der Griechen*, vol. III, pt. 1, (5th ed., Leipzig, 1923), pp. 93–105. On the Stoic categories see also: O. Reith, *Grundbegriffe der Stoischen Ethik* (Berlin, 1933); M. Pohlenz, " Die Begründung der abendländischen Sprachlehre durch die Stoa," *Göttingische gelehrte Nachrichten*, vol. 2 (1938), pp. 182–185; *idem, Die Stoa* (Göttingen, 1949); P. de Lacy, " The Stoic Categories," *Transactions of the American Philological Association*, vol. 76 (1945), pp. 261–263; M. E. Reesor, " The Stoic Concept of Quality," *American Journal of Philology*, vol. 75 (1954), pp. 40–58.

[34] Van den Bergh, *op. cit.*, vol. II, pp. 4–5 (n. 3.6). Cf. footnote 2 above.

[35] *Ibid.*, pp. 136–137 (n. 237.2). Ultimately the discussion of course carries back to Plato's *Sophist* (240b) and its conception of a realm of *meanings* that represent a mode of being intermediate between the actually real and the utterly nonexistent. (Cf. *Theaetetus*, 189a.)

[36] Some Stoics distinguished distinct senses of the term—a narrow sense (*poiotēs*) in which a " quality " can be attributed only to an existent and a wider one (*poion*) in which it can also be applied to nonexistents. Zeller, *op. cit.*, p. 98 (n. 1 *ad* p. 97); Bréhier, *op. cit.*, pp. 8–9.

The Arabic term *ḥāl* ("state") represents the Stoic *pōs echon*.[37] And Arabic *iḍāfah* ("relation") represents the Stoic *pros ti pōs echon*. The Stoics—like the Sceptics and most of the Muʿtazilites—regarded relations as subjective.[38]

The contemporarily popular "modern" view that nonexistent possibles are to be denied any (strictly) ontological status because the foundation on which they rest is purely linguistic finds its counterparts in the medieval Arabic discussions, and indeed comes round in a full circle to the position espoused in classical antiquity by the Stoics in their theory of the *lekta* ("meanings"; Arabic: *maʿānī*).[39]

In general, it may be said that the searching discussions of the concept of existence nowadays proceeding among logicians, like the earlier ones current in medieval Arabic philosophy, represent variations on a Stoic theme.[40]

---

[37] On *ḥāl* see M. Horten, "Die Modus-Theorie des Abu Haschim," *Zeitschrift der deutschen morgenländischen Gesellschaft*, vol. 63 (1909), pp. 303–324 and O. Pretzl, *op. cit.*, pp. 51–54. Thinking only of Aristotle among the ancients, Horten claims that the theory of "states" is an indigeneously Islamic development. On our view of the matter, the circumstantial evidence points almost conclusively to a Stoic origin.

[38] Van den Bergh, *op. cit.*, vol. II, p. 11 (n. 13.1), and p. 81 (n. 119.2).

[39] For *al-maʿnā* (pl. *al-maʿānī*) see O. Pretzl, *op. cit.*, pp. 37–43 and M. Horten, "Was bedeutet *m-ʿ-n-y* als philosophischer Terminus," *Zeitschrift der deutschen morgenländischen Gesellschaft*, vol. 64 (1910), pp. 391–396. Also *idem*, "Die ideenlehre des Muʿammar," *Archiv für systematische Philosophie*, vol. 15 (1909), pp. 469–484. Al-Jubbāʾī's use of the term *al-musammā* is also close to the Stoic *lekton*. Cf. H. Ritter (ed.), *Die dogmatischen Lehren der Anhänger des Islam von Abu l-Hasan ʿAlī ibn Ismāʿīl al-Ashʿarī* (Istanbul, 1929; *Bibliotheca Islamica* I; 2d edition, Wiesbaden, 1963), pp. 158–162. However, none of the authorities cited have remarked the Stoic roots of the concepts at issue.

[40] I wish to thank Dr. Bas van Fraassen who served as my research assistant in the preparation of this study, and am grateful to Mr. Salih Alich for helpful comments on a draft of the paper.

VII

THE THEORY OF TEMPORAL MODALITIES
IN ARABIC LOGIC AND PHILOSOPHY

1. INTRODUCTION

In the wake of A. N. Prior's book on *Time and Modality* [1] an active interest has sprung up among logicians in the logical theory of chronological propositions generally, and particularly in the relationships that obtain between such propositions and modal concepts. This phenomenon is not surprising, because the issue is one that ramifies widely into various topics of logico-philosophical interest: the theory of tensed discourse, the problem of determinism, and the puzzle of future contingency, among others. The modern discussions have gone forward wholly oblivious to the fact that medieval Arabic logicians had given extensive attention to the development of a theory of temporal modalities, and had developed an extensive and subtle machinery for dealing with problems in this area. The aim of the present discussion is one of " intellectual archeology "—to present the Arabic contributions to this branch of logic in such a way that their linkage with ideas and concepts of present-day interest can be assessed and appreciated.

2. SOURCES

The principal basis for our discussion is " The Sun Epistle " *Al-Risālah al-shamsiyyah* of the thirteenth-century Persian philosopher-scientist al-Qazwīnī al-Kātibī [2] (ca. 1220–1276 or 1292). Not only is this work one of the few that treats of our problem in significant

---

[1] Oxford, The Clarendon Press, 1957.
[2] For this Arabic logician—as well as all others to be mentioned here—see the biobibliographical register in N. Rescher, *The Development of Arabic Logic* (Pittsburgh, 1964); see pp. 203–204.

detail, but it is one of the very few Arabic logic treatises to have been put into a European language, as follows: Aloys Sprenger, *Dictionary of the Technical Terms Used in the Sciences of the Musulmans*, Part 2 (Calcutta, 1862). Appendix I (1862) on " The Logic of the Arabians " gives an Arabic text edition and a (somewhat incomplete) English translation of our treatise. This translation has a serious shortcoming from the standpoint of our present concerns. As the translator explains, certain parts of the treatise (to wit, the following sections, Engl. 68–70 = Ar. 66–68; Engl. 72–74 = Ar. 70–72; Engl. 84–86 = Ar. 81–84) " are omitted in the translation because they contain details on modals which are of no interest. The last-named four paragraphs [dealing with modal syllogisms] are also omitted in most Arabic text books on Logic, and not studied in Mohammedan Schools " (p. 25, n. 39). I have presented an English translation of this material in another publication to which the present chapter is substantially indebted: *Temporal Modalities in Arabic Logic* (Dordrecht, 1966; Supplementary Series of *Foundations of Language*). No matter how difficult or boring such considerations may have proved for the Muslim schoolmaster, it is of the greatest relevance for our interests.

It goes perhaps without saying that, although we base our discussion in the main upon the treatise of al-Qazwīnī al-Kātibī, the exposition will draw upon a wider range of Arabic logicians, including such more prominent figures as Avicenna and Averroes. In particular, we shall see that al-Qazwīnī al-Kātibī follows and draws upon Avicenna. Details of this reliance will be obvious at many points to anyone who compares al-Qazwīnī's treatment with the corresponding treatment of Avicenna's *Kitāb al-ishārāt wa-'l-tanbīhāt*, which is fortunately accessible to European scholars in an excellent French version: A. M. Goichon (tr.), *Ibn Sīnā: Livre des Directives et Remarques* (Beyrouth and Paris, 1951). Al-Qazwīnī's dependence upon Avicenna is strikingly evidenced by the close parallelism in organization, mode of treatment, and substance between the two treatises.

3. BACKGROUND

The logic of modality was a relative latecomer to the domain of

Arabic logic. Only after the time of Abū Bishr Mattā ibn Yūnus (ca. 870–940), translator of *Posterior Analytics*, did the study of Aristotle's modal syllogistic come to be taken up.[3] In its wake, interest in other Greek ideas regarding modality sprung up, and in the 10th century there was a lively polemic in the School of Baghdad—whose principal figure was al-Fārābī (ca. 873–950)—against Galen's views on modality, especially his rejection of the modality of possibility.[4] The mainstream of Arabic logic which stayed within the tradition of the School of Baghdad, culminating in Averroes (1126–1198), always remained closely faithful to Aristotelian views.[5] On the other hand, the influence of Galen, and especially—perhaps through his mediation—of the Stoics, made significant headway in that part of the Arabic logical tradition whose fountain-head was Avicenna.[6] There can be little doubt that the theory of temporal modalities with which we shall be dealing in the present monograph goes back, either entirely, or at any rate in its original and generative impetus, to Greek, and above all to Stoic logic. We shall, however, postpone any detailed consideration of the cognate conceptions of Megarian and Stoic until Sect. 13, after our examination of the Arabic materials has been completed.

The theory of temporalized modalities was developed by the Arabs within an Aristotelian setting, against the backdrop of a concept of demonstrative science insisting upon explanations in terms of premisses that are necessary in the sense of comprising constantly operative causes referring to what *always* happens.[7] Consider, for the sake of illustration, Avicenna's statement:

[3] "Al-Fārābī on Logical Tradition" in N. Rescher, *Studies in the History of Arabic Logic* (Pittsburgh, 1963), pp. 21–27.
[4] See N. Rescher, *The Development of Arabic Logic (op. cit.)*, p. 43.
[5] See, for example, "Averroes' *Quaesitum* on Assertoric (Absolute) Propositions" in N. Rescher, *Studies in the History of Arabic Logic (op. cit.)*, pp. 91–105. The extent to which the Spanish Muslim logicians were faithful to Aristotle is exemplified by the treatment of modal syllogistic by Abū 'l-Salt (1068–1134). See "Abū-'l-Salt of Denia on Modal Syllogisms," *ibid.*, pp. 87–90.
[6] See, for example, "Avicenna on the Logic of 'Conditional' Propositions," *ibid.*, pp. 76–86. On the general phenomenon see N. Rescher, *The Development of Arabic Logic (op. cit.)*, pp. 50 ff., and *idem*, *Galen and the Syllogism* (Pittsburgh, 1966), pp. 4–8.
[7] Cf. M. E. Marmura, "Ghazali and Demonstrative Science," *Journal of the History of Philosophy*, vol. 3 (1965), pp. 183–204.

The mind is not at all repelled by the statement, " when Zayd moved his hand, the key moved," or " Zayd moved his hand, then the key moved." The mind is repelled, however, by the statement, " when the key moved, Zayd moved his hand," even though it is [rightly] said, " when the key moved, *we knew that* Zayd moved his hand." The mind, despite the temporal coexistence of the two movements, assigns a (causal) priority for one, a posteriority for the other. For it is not the existence of the second movement that causes the existence of the first; it is the first movement that causes the second.[8]

Its rooting in the fertile soil of the concepts of causality and necessity provided for the Arabs the impetus to preoccupation with the logical theory of temporally modalized propositions.

4. FUNDAMENTAL IDEAS

The theory of modal propositions is superadded to or superimposed upon a basic theory of absolute, unmodalized, categorical propositions (of the standard **A, E, I,** and **O** type). Let us here use the variables

$$A, B, C, \ldots$$

to stand for such categorical propositions.

When a proposition of this sort is modalized, it bears a modal qualifier such as " necessarily," " perpetually," " non-necessarily," or " non-perpetually " (§ 48).[9]

The idea of modality is introduced in § 48 in the following terms:

The relation of the predicates to the subjects must—be they affirmative or negative—have a certain qualification such as " necessarily," " perpetually," " non necessarily," or " non perpetually." Such a qualification is called the *materia* (*maddah*) of the proposition, and the word expressing it, is called the *mode* (*jihah*) of the proposition.

In Avicenna's *Kitāb al-ishārāt wa-'l-tanbīhāt* [10] the same point is put as follows: " By the *materia* [of a proposition] we understand the three states upon which, in the affirmation rests the truth of these

---

[8] *Ibn Sīnā, Al-Shifā': al-Ilāhiyāt (Metaphysics)* (ed. C. G. Anawati, S. Dunya, and S. Zayd, revised by M. Madkur), 2 vols. (Cairo, 1960), vol. I, p. 165.

[9] We adopt the practice of citing in this way the section-numbering adopted in the Sprenger *translation* of our treatise. His numbering of paragraphs in the English version unaccountably differs in places from that used for the Arabic text.

[10] I cite this from the French version of A. M. Goichon, already mentioned above.

three words ['necessary,' 'possible,' 'impossible'] when they are used explicitly" (p. 134). A correspondence theory of modality appears to be at work here: there is an objective kind of fact *de re* correspondence with which constitutes the truth-ground of the modalized proposition *de dicto*. Here and elsewhere (§§ 40, 41, 46) it is maintained that this modality-underwriting fact is one with respect to the sort of relation—and preeminently temporal relation—which obtains between the subject and the predicate.

In the explanation of various modalities, various technical ideas are required as special instruments.

One item of technical equipment is a bracket operator to indicate the subject of a categorical proposition so that

$$[A]$$

represents the subject of (the proposition) A.

Another needed item of technical equipment is an existence operator. This will be represented by '$E!$', so that "$E!X$" says "X exists", and

$$E![A]$$

to be construed as "the essence of the subject of A exists" or perhaps as "the subject of A is actually exemplified." It should be noted that "$E![A]$" is equivalent with "$E![\sim A]$," where $\sim A$ is, of course, the contradictory of A.

5. BASIC MODAL RELATIONS

We shall need to work with four basic modal relationships:

1. $(A/\Box/B)$

for "A is necessarily true whenever B is true." (We shall call this relationship that of *chronologically constant necessity-correlation*.)

2. $(A/\forall t/B)$

for "A is true whenever B is true." (We shall call this relationship that of *chronologically constant correlation*.)

3. $(A/\exists t/B)$

for "A is true at some time that B is true" (*chronologically occasional correlation*).

4. $(A/\Diamond/B)$

for " *A* is possible at some time that *B* is true " (*chronologically occasional possibility-correlation*).

To provide a fuller and more precise explication of the ideas at issue here let us introduce somewhat more symbolic machinery, to wit, t, t', t'', etc., as variables for *times*; $T_t(A)$ for " *A* is true at the time t "; $N_t(A)$ for " *A* is necessarily true at the time t "; $P_t(A)$ for " *A* is possibly true at the time t "; → for entailment or (strict) implication. Now we can construe the four aforementioned relationships as follows (with " iff " as abbreviation for " if and only if "):

1. $(A/\Box/B)$ iff $(\forall t)$ $[T_t(B) \rightarrow N_t(A)]$
2. $(A/\forall t/B)$ iff $(\forall t)$ $[T_t(B) \rightarrow T_t(A)]$
3. $(A/\exists t/B)$ iff $(\exists t)$ $[T_t(A)$ & $T_t(B)]$
4. $(A/\Diamond/B)$ iff $(\exists t)$ $[P_t(A)$ & $T_t(B)]$

If we accept the plausible principle that what is possible under given circumstances at one time is possible under those circumstances at all times, we could indifferently construe (4) as " *A* is possible at all times that *B* is true."

We could clearly adopt only two of these four relationships as primitive ideas, introducing the other two by means of the duality-equivalences

$\sim(A/\Box/B)$ iff $(\sim A/\Diamond/B)$
$\sim(A/\forall t/B)$ iff $(\sim A/\exists t/B)$

Moreover, it is clearly intended that we should have:

If $(A/\Box/B)$, then $(A/\forall t/B)$ [11]

This, of course, is an immediate consequence of the foregoing constructions. And then we also obtain derivatively

If $(A/\exists t/B)$, then $(A/\Diamond/B)$

The affirmativeness or negativeness of a complex of the form $(A/-/-)$ is to be considered as determined by that of *A*.

Thus, to give a specific example of the working of these ideas

(All *S* is $P/\forall t/E![$All *S* is *P*$])$

means: " All *S* is *P* as long as the essence of *S* exists, i.e., as long as there are *S*'s."

This locution " as long as the essence of the subject exists " as it is used in §§ 50–51 appears to mean " throughout the entire history of

[11] Compare St. Thomas Aquinas: *Est igitur Deus aeternus: cum omne necessarium per se sit aeternum.* (*Summa contra Gentiles*, I, c. 15.)

the existence of the subject." For example, the modalized proposition " It is necessary that every man is an animal " is explained as meaning that the predicate of being an animal pertains of necessity to man as long as the essence of the subject exists—i.e., as long as there are men. In § 25 universals are grouped into three classes—physical, logical, and mental—with " animal " as the paradigmatic physical universal[12] said to have the locus of its existence in its instances, that is, in the existence of animals.

It is by means of (not the notations but) the *concepts* here introduced that our author defines the modal " qualifiers " characterizing " the relation of the predicates to the subjects " (§ 48) in modalized categorical propositions.

6. ENUMERATION OF MODAL PROPOSITIONS—

I. SIMPLE MODALITIES

There are six types of simple modal propositions (enumerated in § 50). Their character is as follows:

1. *Type N_A: The Absolute Necessary*

With respect to the *absolute necessary*, the text and examples of § 50.1 make it clear that this modalization of a categorical proposition P is to be construed as amounting to

$$(A/\Box/E![A])$$

that is to say, as asserting that A is necessarily the case as long as the essence of its subject exists (i.e., is exemplified). The text puts the matter as follows, that the proposition so modalized: " pronounces that the predicate is affirmed or denied [of an instance] of the subject of necessity as long as the essence of the subject exists [in this instance] " (§ 50.1).

2. *Type R_A: The Absolute Perpetual*

The *absolute perpetual* proposition is to be construed as

$$(A/\forall t/E![A])$$

that is to say, as asserting that A is perpetually the case as long as—i.e., is always true whenever—the essence of its subject exists

---

[12] The other two types of universals are ruled out of discussion as irrelevant for present purposes.

(i.e., is exemplified). The proposition so modalized: " pronounces that the predicate is affirmed or denied of the subject in perpetuity as long as the essence of the subject exists" (§ 50.2).

3. *Type C_G: The General Conditional (Also: Absolute Temporal)*

The *general conditional* proposition is to be construed as

$$(A/\Box/C[A])$$

that is to say, as asserting that A is necessarily the case as long as its subject satisfies the condition C. It appears (at § 51.5) that this form of modality is also called the *absolute temporal*. The proposition so modalized " pronounces that the predicate is affirmed or denied of necessity [of the subject] under the condition of [the obtaining of] a certain attribute of its subject" (§ 50.3). The example is given that " Every writer moves his fingers as long as he writes (i.e., not at all times, but as long as he is actually a writer)."

4. *Type V_G: The General Conventional (Also: Absolute Spread)*

The *general conventional* proposition is to be construed as

$$(A/\forall t/C[A])$$

that is to say, as asserting that A is perpetually the case as long as its subject satisfies the condition C. The proposition so modalized: " pronounces that the predicate is affirmed or denied of the subject in perpetuity under the condition of [the obtaining of] a certain attribute of its subject " (§ 50.4).

5. *Type A_G: The General Absolute*

The *general absolute* proposition is to be construed as

$$(A/\exists t/E![A]) \text{ or equivalently } \sim(\sim A/\forall t/E![\sim A])$$

that is to say that A is the case at some time, i.e., with its subject term construed to hold *at some time* for all its then concurrently existing instances. The proposition so modalized pronounces that the predicate is actually (or: *at some time*) affirmed or denied of the subject (§ 50.5). The example is given that " Every man is breathing."

Note that—as is claimed at the end of § 51—the general absolute A_G is a contradictory of the absolute perpetual R_A.

6. *Type P_G: The General Possible*

The *general possible* proposition has the form

$$\sim(\sim A/\Box/E![\sim A]) \text{ or equivalently } (A/\Diamond/E![A])$$

that is to say that A is possible as long as (i.e., whenever) the subject of A exists. The proposition so modalized: " pronounces that there is no absolute necessity that what is contrary to the judgment should not be the case " (§ 50.6).

Note again that—as is claimed at the end of § 51—the general possible is a contradictory of the absolute necessary.

To summarize, then, we are presented with six basic types of temporally construed modalized propositions of the *simple* uncompounded variety, as follows:

Code [13]		Name	Construction	
1.	N_A	Absolute necessary	$(A/\Box/E![A])$	" A is necessarily true whenever $E![A]$ "
2.	R_A	Absolute perpetual	$(A/\forall t/E![A])$	" A is perpetually true whenever $E![A]$ "
3.	C_G	General conditional [also " absolute temporal "]	$(A/\Box/C[A])$	" A is necessarily true whenever $C[A]$ "
4.	V_G	General conventional [also " absolute spread "]	$(A/\forall t/C[A])$	" A is perpetually true whenever $C[A]$ "
5.	A_G	General absolute	$(A/\exists t/E![A])$	" A is occasionally true when $E![A]$ "
6.	P_G	General possible	$(A/\Diamond/E![A])$	" A is possibly true when $E![A]$"

7. Enumeration of Modal Propositions—

II. Compound Modalities

Propositions are defined as being compound when " their verity is composed at the same time of an affirmation and a negation " (§ 49).

[13] Two types of modalities which would fit naturally into this framework are not mentioned at all, viz. (i) $(A/\exists t/C[A])$ and (ii) $(A/\Diamond/C[A])$. The reason for this apparent neglect is that these must be construed to amount to (5) and (6) respectively.

Seven compound modal propositions are introduced in our text as follows:

7. *Type C_S:* *The Special Conditional*

The *special conditional* proposition is to be construed as

$$(A/\Box/C[A]) \ \& \ (\sim A/\exists t/E![\sim A])$$

It is, as our text puts it: " the same as the general conditional with the restriction that the relation of the subject [and predicate] is not perpetual in regard to the essence [of the subject] " (§ 51.1). In other words it is the combination of the general conditional with the corresponding negativized absolute perpetual, i.e., with the corresponding negative general absolute. (The affirmativeness or negativeness of the modal proposition turns on that of A.)

8. *Type V_S:* *The Special Conventional*

The *special conventional* proposition is to be construed as

$$(A/\forall t/C[A]) \ \& \ (\sim A/\exists t/E![\sim A])$$

As the texts puts it, it is " the same as the general conventional with the restriction that it [the relation of the subject and predicate] is not perpetual in regard to the essence [of the subject] " (§ 51.2). In other words, it is the combination of the general conventional with the denial of the corresponding absolute perpetual, i.e., with the corresponding negative general absolute. (The affirmativeness or negativeness of the modal proposition again turns on that of A.)

9. *Type $\bar{N}_E$:* *The Non-Necessary Existential*

The *non-necessary existential* proposition is to be construed as

$$(A/\exists t/E![A]) \ \& \ (\sim A/\Diamond/E![\sim A])$$

As the text puts it, it is: " the same as the general absolute with the restriction that it [the relation of the subject and predicate] is not one of necessity in regard to the essence [of the subject] " (§ 51.3). In other words, it is the combination of the general absolute with the denial of the corresponding absolute necessary, i.e., with the corresponding negative general possible.

10. *Type $\bar{R}_E$: The Non-Perpetual Existential*

The *non-perpetual existential* proposition is to be construed as

$$(A/\exists t/E![A]) \ \& \ (\sim A/\exists t/E![\sim A])$$

The text puts it that it is: " the same as the general absolute with the restriction of non-perpetuity in regard to the essence [of the subject] " (§ 51.4). It is thus the combination of the general absolute with the denial of the corresponding absolute perpetual, i.e., with the corresponding negative general absolute. As throughout its affirmativeness and negativeness hinges upon that of A.

11. *Type T: The Temporal*

The *temporal* proposition is to be construed as

$$(A/\square/T[A]) \ \& \ (\sim A/\exists t/E![\sim A])$$

Here $T[A]$ represents a special condition on the subject $[A]$—viz. that we have to do with a certain definite period of its existence. The text puts it that: " it pronounces that the predicate is affirmed or denied of the subject of necessity during a definite period of the existence of the subject, under the restriction of non-perpetuity in regard to the essence of the subject " (§ 51.5). In other words, it is the combination of the absolute temporal (so the text!) with the denial of the absolute perpetual, i.e., with the corresponding negative general absolute.

12. *Type S: The Spread*

The *spread* proposition is to be construed as

$$(A/\square/S[A]) \ \& \ (\sim A/\exists t/E![\sim A])$$

Here $S[A]$ represents a special condition on the subject $[A]$—viz. that have to do with some indefinite period of its existence.

Out text puts it that: " it pronounces that the predicate is affirmed or denied of the subject of necessity during an indefinite period of the existence of the subject, under the restriction of non-perpetuity in reference to the essence [of the subject] " (§ 51.6). In other words, it is the combination of the absolute spread (so the text!) corresponding negative general absolute.

13. *Type P_S: The Special Possible*

The *special possible*—also *contingent*—proposition is to be construed as

$$(A/\Diamond/E![A]) \ \& \ (\sim A/\Diamond/E![\sim A])$$

In other words, it is the combination of a general possible with the corresponding negativized general possible. As the text puts it, the special possible: " pronounces that there is no absolute necessity either for the existence or non-existence of the relation. . . . It is composed of two general possible propositions, one of which is affirmative and the other negative " (§ 51.7). As the text rightly observes, there is, in such propositions, no difference between the affirmative and the negative form.

* * *

To summarize, then, we are presented with seven basic types of temporally construed modalized propositions of the *compound* variety, as follows:

		Construction	
Code	Name	Affirmative Component	Negative Component
7. C_S	Special conditional	$(A/\Box/C[A])$	$(\sim A/\exists t/E![\sim A])$
8. V_S	Special conventional	$(A/\forall t/C[A])$	$(\sim A/\exists t/E![\sim A])$
9. $\bar{N}_E$	Non-necessary existential	$(A/\exists t/E![A])$	$(\sim A/\Diamond/E![\sim A])$
10. $\bar{R}_E$	Non-perpetual existential	$(A/\exists t/E![A])$	$(\sim A/\exists t/E![\sim A])$
11. T	Temporal	$(A/\Box/T[A])$	$(\sim A/\exists t/E![\sim A])$
12. S	Spread	$(A/\Box/S[A])$	$(\sim A/\exists t/E![\sim A])$
13. P_S	Special possible	$(A/\Diamond/E![A])$	$(\sim A/\Diamond/E![\sim A])$

Basically only five distinct modalities are involved here, (11) and (12) both being capable of being viewed as special cases of (7).

A word must be said about the completeness of this enumeration. Let us dismiss (11) and (12) on the grounds adduced. Let it be that the negative component must either take the form $(\sim A/\exists t/E![\sim A])$ or $(\sim A/\Diamond/E![\sim A])$. Then twelve theoretical possibilities confront us, as follows:

Affirmative Component	Negative Component	Remarks
1a. $(A/\square/E![A])$	$(\sim A/\exists t/E![\sim A])$	cannot arise
1b. ,,	$(\sim A/\lozenge/E![\sim A])$	cannot arise
2a. $(A/\forall t/E![A])$	$(\sim A/\exists t/E![\sim A])$	cannot arise
2b. ,,	$(\sim A/\lozenge/E![\sim A])$	(α)
3a. $(A/\square/C[A])$	$(\sim A/\exists t/E![\sim A])$	= case 7
3b. ,,	$(\sim A/\lozenge/E![\sim A])$	cannot arise
4a. $(A/\forall t/C[A])$	$(\sim A/\exists t/E![\sim A])$	= case 8
4b. ,,	$(\sim A/\lozenge/E![\sim A])$	(β)
5a. $(A/\exists t/E![A])$	$(\sim A/\exists t/E![\sim A])$	= case 10
5b. ,,	$(\sim A/\lozenge/E![\sim A])$	= case 9
6a. $(A/\lozenge/E![A])$	$(\sim A/\exists t/E![\sim A])$	(γ)
6b. ,,	$(\sim A/\lozenge/E![\sim A])$	= case 13

There are, on first view, three seeming gaps in the enumeration, which we have labeled (α)–(γ) in the *Remarks* column. If, however, we adopt the principle that what is possible must happen sometimes, viz.

$$(A/\lozenge/-) \rightarrow (A/\exists t/-)$$

we can at once eliminate (α) and (β) from the sphere of feasibility. Moreover, case (6a) reduces to (5b) when we put ' $\sim A$ ' for ' A ': thus (6a) does not represent an independent concatenation, and the omission of (γ) is apparent rather than real. This indicates the essential completeness of the system.

We thus arrive at the following set of temporalized modalities whose coherence and completeness may now be regarded as established:

Name	Code	Construction	Type [14]
1. Absolute necessary	N_A	$(A/\square/E![A])$	N (necessary)
2. Absolute perpetual	R_A	$(A/\forall t/E![A])$	A (assertoric)
3. General conditional	C_G	$(A/\square/C[A])$	N
4. General conventional	V_G	$(A/\forall t/C[A])$	A
5. General absolute	A_G	$(A/\exists t/E![A])$	P (possible)
6. General possible	P_G	$(A/\lozenge/E![A])$	P
7. Special conditional	C_S	$(A/\square/C[A])$ & $(\sim A/\exists t/E![\sim A])$	N
8. Special conventional	V_S	$(A/\forall t/C[A])$ & $(\sim A/\exists t/E![A])$	A

[14] Cf. the discussion of Sect. 12 below.

Name	Code	Construction	Type
9. Non-necessary existential $\bar{N}_E$		$(A/\exists t/E![A])$ & $(\sim A/\Diamond/E![\sim A])$	P
10. Non-perpetual existential $\bar{R}_E$		$(A/\exists t/E![A])$ & $(\sim A/\exists t/E![\sim A])$	P
11. Temporal	T	$(A/\Box/T[A])$ & $(\sim A/\exists t/E![\sim A])$	N
12. Spread	S	$(A/\Box/S[A])$ & $(\sim A/\exists t/E![\sim A])$	N
13. Special possible	P_S	$(A/\Diamond/E![A])$ & $(\sim A/\Diamond/E![\sim A])$	P

8. Rules for Contradictories

These rules, as stated in § 60 for the simple modal proposition are as shown in the next given tabulation. It is curious that the last two cases (5) and (6) are wholly omitted in the discussion of § 60.

Original Name	Construction	Contradictory Construction	Name
1. Absolute necessary	$(A/\Box/E![A])$	$(\sim A/\Diamond/E![\sim A])$	General possible
2. Absolute perpetual	$(A/\forall t/E![A])$	$(\sim A/\exists t/E![\sim A])$	General absolute
3. General conditional	$(A/\Box/C[A])$	$(\sim A/\Diamond/E![\sim A])$	General possible *
4. General conventional	$(A/\forall t/C[A])$	$(\sim A/\exists t/E![\sim A])$	General absolute †
5. General absolute	$(A/\exists t/E![A])$	$(\sim A/\forall t/E![\sim A])$	Absolute perpetual
6. General possible	$(A/\Diamond/E![A])$	$(\sim A/\Box/E![\sim A])$	Absolute necessary

* Possible temporal in the text: perhaps for $(\sim A/\Diamond/C[\sim A])$.
† Absolute temporal in the text: perhaps for $(\sim A/\exists t/C[\sim A])$.

The rules for the contradictories of compound modal propositions are stated in §§ 61–62 as follows: The complex modal proposition consists of (1) a simple modal proposition as its base, and (2) a correspondingly negativized rider which is either a general absolute or a general possible. To form its contradictory we

    i. Form the contradictory of its modal base, and
    ii. Disjoin it with the contradictory of its rider.

Thus by this rule the contradictory of the non-perpetual existential

$$(A/\exists t/E![A]) \ \& \ (\sim A/\exists t/E![\sim A])$$

would be
$$(\sim\!A/\forall t/E![\sim\!A]) \text{ v } (A/\forall t/E![A])$$
that is a disjunction of two absolute perpetuals. The theory of contradictories is not dealt with very thoroughly in our text, which can, however, be supplemented by other sources. (See ch. VIII below.)

9. Conversion (i.e., Simple Conversion)

The treatment of conversion (*conversio simplex*) for categorical propositions—as described in § 64—is, of course, routine and straightforward: " ' Even conversion ' (i.e., simple conversion) is an expression which means that the first part [i.e., *term*] of a proposition is put second and the second part first, and that the truth and *quale* remain unaltered " (§ 64). The situation is as follows:

	Original	Converse
A	All S is P	Some P is S [" limitation "]
E	No S is P	No P is S
I	Some S is P	Some P is S
O	Some S is not P	Some P is not S [INVALID]

In asking for the converse of a modalized proposition $(A/-/-)$, what we are after is another modalized proposition $(B/-/-)$ such that: (1) B is the converse of A, and (2) this second modalized proposition, involving B, is a valid consequence of the first, involving A.

Consider, for the sake of an example, the **E** proposition *No S is P* modalized as an absolute perpetual
$$(\text{No } S \text{ is } P/\forall t/E!S)$$
From this it immediately follows that
$$(\text{No } P \text{ is } S/\forall t/E!S)$$
Now if we are entitled to assume that S and P are " temporally coordinate "—i.e., that E!S whenever E!P, and conversely—we can infer
$$(\text{No } P \text{ is } S/\forall t/E!P)$$
which is the absolute perpetual for the converse of our original **E** proposition. This illustrates the process of conversion (i.e., simple conversion) among modalized propositions—and also illustrates its dependence upon an assumption of " temporal coordination." [15]

---

[15] For details regarding the claims made by our author with respect to conversion, see N. Rescher, *Temporal Modalities in Arabic Logic* (*op. cit.*).

95

Our author's discussion of the conversion of modal propositions is in substance very close to—though not wholly identical with—that of Bar Hebraeus (also derived from Avicenna) as presented in a form conveniently accessible to the non-orientalist in H. F. Janssens, *L'Entretien de la Sagesse de Bar Hebraeus* (Liège and Paris, 1937; Bibliothèque de la Faculté de Philosophie et des Lettres de l'Université de Liège, fasc. LXXV), pp. 186–193. For details, the next-given tabulation should be consulted.

THE SIMPLE CONVERSION OF MODAL PROPOSITIONS ACCORDING TO BAR HEBRAEUS [1]

	Original	*Converse*	
A *Propositions and* **I** *Propositions*			
1. Absolute [2] (i.e., general absolute)	All *S* is *P* / Some *S* is *P*	Some *P* is *S*	Absolute
2. Necessary (i.e., absolute necessary)	Some *S* is *P*	Some *P* is *S*	Absolute [3]
3. Special possible	All *S* is *P* / Some *S* is *P*	Some *P* is *S*	General possible
4. Perpetual (permanent)	(case not discussed)		
5. Temporal	(case not discussed)		
O *Propositions*			
None convertible at all.[5]			
E *Propositions*			
1. Absolute (i.e., general absolute)	No *S* is *P*	not convertible	
3. Necessary (i.e., absolute necessary)	No *S* is *P*	No *P* is *S*	Necessary [6]
3. Special possible	No *S* is *P*	not convertible	
4. Perpetual (permanent)	No *S* is *P*	No *P* is *S*	Perpetual
5. Temporal	No *S* is *P*	not convertible	

[1] From H. F. Janssens (ed.), *L'Entretien de la Sagesse de Bar Hebraeus* (Liège and Paris, 1937; Bibliothèque de la Faculté de Philosophie et des Lettres de l'Université de Liège, fasc. LXXV), pp. 186–193.

[2] This is apparently what we know from al-Qazwīnī al-Kātibī as the *general absolute* ($A/\exists t/E![A]$), and not the " absolute " in the sense of the unmodalized or strictly assertoric.

[3] In al-Qazwīnī al-Kātibī, this is not the (general) absolute, but the " absolute temporal " (§ 69).

[4] According to al-Qazwīnī al-Kātibī, this conversion is " unknown " (§ 70).

[5] So far as the types of modality at issue are concerned, this agrees with al-Qazwīnī al-Kātibī. But compare Table IV above.

[6] According to al-Qazwīnī al-Kātibī (§ 66), this is not the (absolute) necessary, but the absolute *perpetual*.

10. C-CONVERSION

(CONVERSION BY CONTRADICTION)

The logical process of *conversion by contradiction* is described in the following terms: " This expression [' conversion by contradiction '] means: to place the contradictory of the second part of a proposition first, and the first part, unaltered, second. The *quale* of the new proposition will be the opposite of the original proposition, but it will be equally true " (§ 71). The workings of this process may be indicated by the following tabulation:

	Original	C-Converse
A	All S is P	No non-P is S
E	No S is P	Some non-P is S [" limitation "]
I	Some S is P	Some non-P is not S [INVALID]
O	Some S is not P	Some non-P is S

The process of C-conversion appears to call for three steps: (1) change S to non-P, (2) change P to S, and (3) change the *quality* of the proposition: in short, the C-converse of a categorical proposition is its converted obverse. Thus in asking for the C-converse of a modalized proposition $(A/-/-)$ what we are after is another modalized proposition $(B/-/-)$ such that: (1) B is the converse of A, and (2) this second modalized proposition, involving B, is a valid consequence of the first, involving A.

Consider, for the sake of an example, the **A** proposition *All S is P* modalized as an absolute perpetual

(All S is $P/\forall t/E!S$)

From this it immediately follows that

(No non-P is $S/\forall t/E!S$)

Now if we are entitled to assume that S and *non-P* are " temporally coordinate "—i.e., that $E!S$ whenever $E!$non-P, and conversely—we can infer

(No non-P is $S/\forall t/E!$non-P)

which is the absolute-perpetual for the C-converse of our original **A** proposition. This illustrates the process of C-conversion (i.e., conversion by contradiction) among modalized propositions. (Again, it also illustrates the dependency of this process upon an assumption of "temporal coordination.") [16]

11. Modal Syllogisms

Rules for determining the modality of the conclusion of syllogisms (that is, assertorically valid syllogisms) with modalized premises are presented in §§ 84–87. Take for example the AAA-1 (*Barbara*) syllogism with a necessary absolute major and a general conditional minor:

$$N_A: \text{All } M \text{ is } P \qquad (\text{All } M \text{ is } P/\square/E!M)$$
$$\underline{C_G: \text{All } S \text{ is } M \qquad (\text{All } S \text{ is } M/\square/C[S])}$$
$$?\ : \text{All } S \text{ is } P \qquad (\text{All } S \text{ is } P/?/?)$$

Note that when $C(S)$ we must have it that $E!S$, and that therefore—since *All S is M*—the condition $E!M$ must be satisfied. Thus the given premises warrant the conclusion

$$(\text{All } S \text{ is } P/\square/C(S))$$

which is a general conditional. Again, it is clear by analogous reasoning that an AAA-1 (*Barbara*) syllogism with two absolute perpetual premises must yield an absolute perpetual conclusion. These examples show the process of syllogistic inference among modalized propositions.

It must be admitted that in working out this theory of modal syllogisms, al-Qazwīnī al-Kātibī commits various serious errors of omission and commission.[17] Considering the intricacy and complexity of the reasoning even with the aid of modern symbolic techniques, this fact should not be viewed as surprising. Indeed, one cannot but admire the fortitude of the old logicians in tackling these problems with the crude representational methods at their disposal.

12. Avicenna as the Source of al-Qazwīnī al-Kātibī's Logic of Modality

In Avicenna's *Kitāb al-ishārāt*,[18] a treatment of modalities is given

---

[16] For details regarding the claims made by our author with respect to *C*-conversion, see N. Rescher, *Temporal Modalities in Arabic Logic* (*op. cit.*).

[17] For details see N. Rescher, *Temporal Modalities in Arabic Logic* (*op. cit.*).

[18] *Kitāb al-ishārāt wa-'l-tanbīhāt* tr. A. M. Goichon, *Ibn Sīnā : Livre des Directives et Remarques* (Beyrouth and Paris, 1951).

which may instructively be compared with that of our treatise. As regards the various kinds of necessity, the situation is as follows:

Avicenna	*al-Qazwīnī*
(P. 134) Every proposition is *either* absolute [i.e., unmodalized], of general application, and a judgment is expressed in it without mention of its necessity, nor of its duration, nor of any other temporal circumstance, nor according to possibility	§ 48 [the absolute or unmodalized]
or something of this sort is expressed in it: necessity, or duration without necessity, or [actual] existence without either duration or necessity.	§ 48 [the modalized]
(1) Necessity sometimes occurs in a categorical [or unqualified] sense, as in the statement " God—be he exalted—exists "; and sometimes necessity is (p. 135) attached to a condition. The condition may be *either*	[not considered: the *categorically* or *unqualifiedly* necessary]
(2) the [entire] duration of the existence of the essence [of the subject]. Thus consider: " Man is necessarily a being that speaks." We do not mean here that man never has ceased nor will cease to be a being that speaks—which would be false of each human being—rather we mean that as long as he remains a human being in his essence, he is a being capable of speech. . . .	the absolute necessary (§ 50.1)
(3) *Or* this condition may be the duration of the state in which the subject remains qualifiable by certain qualities which it posses [i.e., the subject may be such that it must of necessity be subject to the predicate as long as it (the subject) remains under a certain condition]. . . .	the general conditional (§ 50.3)
(4) The case is different . . . [when] a condition is applicable to subjects [under a limitation of non-perpetuity]	the special conditional (§ 51.1)
(5) So that it applies (p. 136) neither for a fixed time, as with an eclipse,	the temporal (§ 51·5)
(6) nor for one that is left indeterminate, as with respiration.	the spread (§ 51.6)

It should be noted that these six modes of necessity include all five of al-Qazwīnī's thirteen modalities which take the form $(A/\square/-)$ with or without the qualification of non-perpetuity $(\sim A/\exists t/E![A])$. It warrants note that Averroes' critical discussion states that in the

99

Kitāb al-shifā' Avicenna treated just these five modes of necessity,[19] namely numbers (1)–(6) with a conflation of the first two.

Turning now to the various kinds of possibility, we find the following situation:

Avicenna	*al-Qazwīnī*
(P. 138) By " possibility " we understand	
(1 a) either that which goes with the negation of [the fact] that necessity of [its] non-existence —that is to say (p. 139) impossibility in the primary and general sense of the term—is to be (p. 140) attributed to the subject . . .	the general possible (§ 50.6)
(1 b) or one understands that which goes with the conjoint negation of the necessity of the non-existence and the necessity of the existence of the subject . . . so that it is possible that it be and possible that it not be, i.e., not impossible that it be and not impossible that it not be.	the special possible (§ 51.7)
(2) (P. 141) . . . this [second] sense of " possible " includes the thing whose existence is not perpetual even if it is necessary some of the time, as an eclipse.	the general absolute (§ 50.5)
(3) The " possible " is sometimes given a third sense. [Here] the judgment is not [strictly] necessary at all—neither at a given time, as with the eclipse, nor under certain circumstances, as with change for that which moves —but it is [actual at some times and not others], as happens with writing for man.	the non-perpetual existential (§ 51.4) and the non-necessary existential (§ 51.3)
(4) Sometimes one understands it [the possible] in yet another sense. In this case one looks to a relation [of the subject to the predicate] which does not belong to the thing at issue at any as yet realized (actualized) stage of its existence, neither by affirmation nor negation. Rather, one looks to its [the subjects] state in the future.	[not considered: the future contingent]

It appears that Avicenna's senses of " possibility " correspond in substance to five further members of al-Qazwīnī al-Kātibī's list of thirteen modalities. These are just the five which possess, in our symbolism, either of the forms

$$(A/\Diamond/-) \text{ or } (A/\exists t/-)$$

<hr/>

[19] See " Averroes' *Quaesitum* on Assertoric Propositions " in N. Rescher, *Studies in the History of Arabic Logic* (*op. cit.*), pp. 91–105 (see § 11 on p. 103).

with or without an amendment of non-perpetuity $(\sim A/\lozenge/E![A])$ or $(\sim A/\exists t/E![A])$.

Furthermore in discussing (on pp. 144–145) the modal determinations of the **A** proposition " All C is B " Avicenna distinguishes three further possibilities, namely that the relationship may be asserted (i) invariably as long as the subject really exists, but without necessity (ii) always under certain definite circumstances (iii) at certain times when the subject really exists, though not perpetually. It appears that these three modes correspond to the absolute perpetual (§ 50.2), the general conventional (§ 50.4), and the special conventional (§ 51.2), respectively. These three different modes of actuality—that is, *assertoric* modalities—have the feature of being represented, in our symbolism, by expressions of the form

$$(A/\forall t/-)$$

with or without an amendment of non-perpetuity $(\sim A/\exists t/ E![\sim A])$.

Thus, not only does Avicenna treat the thirteen modalities of al-Qazwīnī, but he classifies them into three groups, as follows:[4]

Modes of Necessity	Modes of Actuality	Modes of Possibility
Absolute necessary	Absolute-perpetual	General absolute
General conditional	General conventional	General possible
Special conditional	Special conventional	Non-necessary
Temporal		existential
Spread		Non-perpetual
		existential
		Special possible

Avicenna's arch-critic, Averroes, rejects this complicated machinery as unwarranted and unnecessary.[20] Averroes affords one interesting historical datum. According to him, Avicenna maintained in the *Kitāb al-shifā'* that Alexander of Aphrodisias construed necessity to include only the first two of these modes— i.e., the absolute necessary and the general conditional—and that, accordingly class the other three modalities of the first group (viz. the special conditional, the temporal, and the spread) as types of actuality. Be this as it may, Averroes himself gives a—to be sure

[20] *Ibid.*, §§ 11–13.

significantly simplified—temporal construction of modalities, presented in a square of opposition as follows: [21]

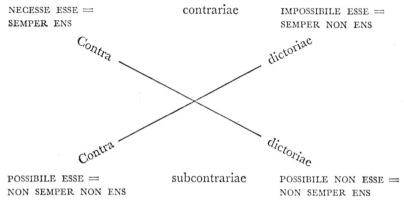

NECESSE ESSE =
SEMPER ENS

contrariae

IMPOSSIBILE ESSE =
SEMPER NON ENS

POSSIBILE ESSE =
NON SEMPER NON ENS

subcontrariae

POSSIBILE NON ESSE =
NON SEMPER ENS

13. TEMPORAL MODALITIES AMONG THE ANCIENT GREEKS

The early history of temporal quantifiers like " sometimes " and " always," and of the theory of temporalized modalities is that linked to them through the mediation of such principles as " What is sometimes actual is always possible " remains shrouded in obscurity. We know that the rudiments of such a theory was actively developed by the ancient Greeks: the Megarians and the Stoics,[22] and Aristotle and the early Peripatetics.[23] The notions of temporalized modality that are at work here are mainly those relating to the " Master Argument " of Diodorus Cronus.[24]

There seems to have been a disagreement as to modality between the Stoics and the Megarians. On the Megarian view:

(1) The *true* is that which is actually realized *now*, so that, using R_t as operator for chronological realization, so that "$R_t(p)$" stands for " p is realized at the time t,"

$$T_n(p) \text{ iff } R_n(p)$$

[21] Averroes, *In I De Caelo*, t. 5, f. 85A.
[22] See E. Zeller, *Die Philosophie der Griechen*, pt. 3, vol. I (5th ed., Leipzig, 1923); and B. Mates, *Stoic Logic* (Berkeley and Los Angeles, 1953), see esp. pp. 36–41.
[23] I. M. Bocheński, *La logique de Théophraste* (Freiburg, 1947).
[24] See Mates, *op. cit.*, pp. 38–39. Cf. J. Hintikka, " Aristotle and the ' Master Argument ' of Diodorus," *American Philosophical Quarterly* vol. I (1964) pp. 101–114. And see also N. Rescher, " A Version of the ' Master Argument ' of Diodorus," *The Journal of Philosophy*, vol. 63 (1966), pp. 438–445.

with $n = now$, or more generally
$$T_t(p) \text{ iff } R_t(p)$$
(2) The *possible* is that which is actually realized (i.e., true) at some present-or-future time
$$P_n(p) \text{ iff } (\exists t)[t \geq n \ \& \ R_n(p)]$$
or more generally
$$P_t(p) \text{ iff } (\exists t')[t' \geq t \ \& \ R_t'(p)]$$
(3) The necessary is that which is actually realized at every future time
$$\mathcal{N}_n(p) \text{ iff } (\jmath A)[t \geq n \rightarrow R_n(p)]$$
or more generally
$$\mathcal{N}_t(p) \text{ iff } (\forall t')[t' \geq t \rightarrow R_t'(p)]$$
The Stoics, on the other hand, dropped the now-relativization of the modalities of possibility and necessity, retaining it only for truth (actuality):

(1) The *time* is that which is actually realized *now*
$$T_n(p) \text{ iff } R_n(p)$$
(2) The *possible* is that which is actually realized at *some* (i.e., any) time
$$P(p) \text{ iff } (\exists t)R_t(p)$$
(3) The *necessary* is that which is actually realized at *all* times
$$\mathcal{N}(p) \text{ iff } (\forall t)R_t(p)$$

Aristotle's position is in line with that of the Stoics in viewing the necessary as that which is true all of the time,[25] a position faithfully reflected in St. Thomas Aquinas' statement that: *Et sic quidquid semper est, non contingenter semper est, sed ex necessitate.*[26]

In all of this there is no limit of the ramified machinery of temporalized modalities which we find in Arabic texts—and which are unquestionably of Greek provenience. For the roots of this theory we must undoubtedly look to the Stoic doctrine of predication. The Stoics distinguished between three types of qualities:

$$
\textit{Poion} \text{ (quality)}
\begin{cases}
\text{i. } \textit{poiotēs} \text{ (permanent property)} \\
\text{ii. } \textit{schēsis} \text{ (enduring state)} \\
\text{iii. } \textit{hexis} \text{ (transient characteristic)}
\end{cases}
$$

[25] J. Hintikka, *op. cit.* Cf. N. Rescher, " Truth and Necessity in Temporal Perspective," in R. M. Gale (ed.), *The Philosophy of Time* (New York, 1967).
[26] *In I De Caelo*, lect. 26, n. 258. And correspondingly: *quod possible est non esse, quandoque non est (Summa Theologica*, IA, q. 2, a. 3). Cf. Guy Jalbert, *Nécessité et contingence chez saint Thomas d'Aquin et chez ses prédécésseurs* (Ottawa, 1961), pp. 204–206, 224–225, and 228.

In construing " quality " (*to poion*) here, we are to work from the top down, and thus have three possibilities: [27]

(1) Only group (i): those qualities that are wholly completed and altogether permanent (*apartizontas kai emmonous ontas*).

(2) Groups (i) and (ii): not only the permanent qualities (e.g., a man's " being an animal ") but the enduring states as well (e.g., " being prudent ").

(3) Groups (i)–(iii): adding to (2) also strictly transient qualities (e.g., " walking " or " running ").

The distinction between such types of qualities lends itself readily to temporalization in the interpretation of propositions in which they are attributed

A man is an animal *all of the time.*
A prudent man acts wisely *most of the time.*
A healthy man walks *some of the time.*

Distinctions of this sort ultimately derive from Aristotle, who in ch. viii of the *Categories* distinguishes between *states* and *conditions* on the basis that states are more stable and enduring (" is just " vs. " is ill " or again " knows Greek " vs. " is speaking Greek ").

The elaboration of such temporalized predications would lend itself naturally to the development of temporal modalities of the sort we have here investigated on the basis of discussions in Arabic logical texts.

It has been known for more than two centuries that there exists in the fine collection of Arabic manuscripts in the Escorial library near Madrid a group of Arabic translations of treatises by Alexander of Aphrodisias, including his refutation of Galen's treatise on possibility. These treatises are reported in Casiri's catalog of 1760,[28] and figure in many later bibliographies.[29]

[27] I follow E. Zeller, *op. cit.*, pp. 97–99 (especially n. 1 for p. 97); relying also upon Émile Bréhier, *La Théorie des incorporels dans l'ancien Stoïcisme* (2d ed., Paris, 1928), p. 9.

[28] Michael Casiri, *Bibliotheca Arabico-Hispana Escurialensis*, 2 vols. (Madrid, 1760–1770); see vol. I, p. 242, codex no. 794 (the Galen refutation is part of the second part of the codex, folios 59–69). In the later catalog of H. Derenbourg and H. P. J. Renaud (*Les manuscrits arabes de l'Escurial* [Paris, 1941]), this codex becomes no. 798.

[29] J. G. Wenrich, *De auctorum graecorum versionibus et commentariis*, etc. (Leipzig, 1842), p. 276. L. Leclerc, *Histoire de la medicine arabe*, vol. I (Paris, 1876), pp. 216–217; M. Steinschneider, *Die Arabischen Uebersetzungen aus dem Griechischen* (Leipzig, 1893; XII Beiheft zum *Centralblatt für Bibliothekswesen*), pp. 93–97, and his earlier *Al-Fārābī* (St. Petersbourg, 1869), p. 93.

The translation we present below is made from the aforementioned unicum manuscript of the Escorial of Alexander of
Aphrodisias' " Refutation of Galen on the Possible." [30] However,
the composite nature of the Escorial manuscript is clearly indicated
by the fact that its *incipit* reads " The treatise of Alexander of
Aphrodisias in refutation of Galen's discourse on the possible "
whereas its *explicit* reads " Alexander's treatise in reply to Galen
concerning the first mover is ended." In fact, the first page alone
deals with possibility (only) and the whole (self-contained) remainder
—written in the same hand—deals with the theory of motion. It is
clear that the Escorial manuscript, rather than presenting a composite treatise, is unquestionably such that two distinct but
juxtaposed works were somehow shuffled together (a thing by no
means impossible in view of the casual conditions which prevailed at
the Escorial for many years in the handling of Arabic manuscripts). [31]
The beginning of the treatise on motion is clearly missing, and
also—alas—all but the initial folio of the treatise on possibility.

The Escorial manuscript of Alexander's treatise on Galen on the
first mover contains at its outset a single manuscript page (folio 59
verso) of Alexander's treatise on Galen on possibility. This one page—
the Arabic text of which has been presented elsewhere [32]—consists
almost entirely of a single long quotation from Galen's (lost) treatise
De possibilitate. This is the only portion of this treatise that is known
to have survived. [33]

The Galen-fragment at issue is, in fact, of considerable interest for
the history of logic. It is well known that Aristotle (and some of the

[30] The scribe of the Escorial MS is Abū 'l-Ḥunain ibn Ibrāhīm ibn Yazīd
al-Kātib. We know nothing else of him. His name is given as the scribe of the
(irrelevant) material page of our MS, but certain identification is possible because
of the uniformity of the script.
[31] See the introductory remarks of Derenbourg's catalog. Indeed it is not
inconceivable that the remainder of the treatise on possibility will yet turn up in
the Escorial, somehow misfiled.
[32] N. Rescher and M. E. Marmura, *The Refutation by Alexander of Aphrodisias of
Galen's Treatise on the Theory of Motion* (Karachi, 1967; Publications of the Central
Institute of Islamic Research).
[33] See the survey of Arabic Alexander MSS in Albert Dietrich, *Die Arabische
Version einer unbekannten Schrift des Alexander von Aphrodisias über die Differentia
specifica, Nachrichten der Akademie der Wissenschaften in Göttingen: Philologisch-historische
Klasse* (Jahrgang 1964), no. 2 (see p. 96, item 11). Here the references to the
treatise by the Arabic biobibliographers are also listed.

Stoic logicians) proposed to construe the modality of *necessity* in terms of *omnitemporality* (construing, for example, " Water is *necessarily* wet " as " Water is wet *at all times*). And as we have seen, the Arabic logicians carried this temporal construction of modality to far greater lengths, elaborating with great sophistication upon the fundamental Aristotelian linkage of modality to time, based on the idea that the necessary is that which happens all of the time.

Now the surprising fact to be gleaned from Galen's report in the fragment here at issue is that *this development of a ramified linkage between time and modality heretofore encountered no earlier than in Arabic logical texts goes back to the earliest Peripatetics*, i.e., to Theophrastus and his followers, who distinguished exactly between rigidly Aristotelian *omnitemporal* necessity (of the " Water is necessarily wet " type described above) and al-Qazwīnī al-Kātibī's " absolute necessity " (of the type: " A man is necessarily an animal " = " A man is an animal so long as he exists ").[34] This early linkage of time and modality is a fact of which we have therefore had only somewhat indirect hints, such as that of the following passage from Alexander's *Commentary on " Prior Analytics "*: " For according to him [Aristotle] the necessary is also predicated of the actual (or: *existent*), for what is actually (or: *existentially*) true of something necessarily belongs to (literally: *exists in*) it, so long as it exists. Thus Theophrastus in the first Book of his *Prior Analytics*, speaking of the meanings of the necessary, writes as follows: ' The third meaning is the existent: for when it exists, it is impossible for it not to exist ' (fr. 58 Wimmer) " (Ed. M. Wallies, 156: 27–157: 2).

In this way, our Galen fragment offers a new datum of considerable interest for the history of modal logic.

TRANSLATION

The Treatise of Alexander of Aphrodisias in Refutation of Galen's Discourse the Possible. [59b1] *Transcribed by Abū 'l-Ḥunain ibn Ibrāhīm ibn on Yazīd al-Kātib.*

Galen said: " The meaning that is understood by the expression ' necessary,' though present in both statements together, /5/ that is,

[34] For a comparable distinction absolutely perpetual motion (" of the eternal everlasting things ") and the non-absolutely perpetual motion (" of things which are not eternal and everlasting but which continue to move as long as they return their nature ") see the treatise on the prime mover, E68a12–14.

in the statement ' The sun shines necessarily ' and also the statement ' Man is rational necessarily ' is one and the same. This is so because the expression ' necessary ' in both these statements refers to no other thing than [the fact] that light exists [invariably] for the sun and rationality for man, an existence which is inseparable. The followers of Theophrastus erred in differentiating between the two things posited as subjects in the two premisses, ' transferring ' to the unknown [35] the predicate /10/ in both things.[36] Since the sun is eternal, [and so also its light], whereas rationality in [man] becomes corruptible by reason of his corruptibility, they [i.e., the followers of Theophrastus] imagined that the necessary has therefore two meanings.[37] In this, their state resembles the state of someone who sees that ' the sensitive ' is at one time predicable of the short, at another of the tall, then of the great, the small, the hardy, the weak, and imagines that sensation differs according to the differences between these things so as to say that some sensation is at one time tall, /15/ some at another time short, some hardy, some weak, some great, some small. Thus just as one who divides sensation along these lines has wrought a bad thing by not investigating the expression ' sensation ' to see in what meaning or meanings it refers to these things—saying that it refers to many diverse things in as much as the meanings it refers to are found in many diverse things—similarly, whoever [38] divides /20/ the necessary into something which is eternal and into something which exists as long as [the thing it refers to] exists, has wrought a bad thing. For he has taken something which is inseparable and divided it according to the differences among the things wherein it exists."

*   *   *

[35] On " transfer to the unknown " see N. Rescher, *Al-Fārābī's Short Commentary on Aristotle's " Prior Analytics "* (Pittsburgh, 1963), pp. 93–98, 108–111.

[36] Presumably this means that since " necessary " is given two senses, we do not know which of the two is operative in a given predication until we look at the subject to see whether it is temporary or eternal; whereas if " necessary " has but one *modus operandi* we can always know how it is used in a given case.

[37] Also apparently the Stoics. *Vide* C. Prantl, *Geschichte der Logik im Abendlande*, vol. I (Leipzig, 1855), pp. 567–568. Actually, Galen holds, the mode of temporal necessity uniform in the two cases, since the predicate pertains always to the subject (throughout its existence—be it temporarily on the one hand or omni-temporally on the other).

[38] Presumably " the followers of Theophrastus." And also the Stoics?

To summarize the situation as regards the theory of temporal modalities among the ancient Greeks, it would seem that the doctrine had its start among the Megarians, and was developed by the Stoics. But the sophisticated logical form of the theory that we find among the Arabs apparently traces its ancestry from Theophrastus and the early Peripatetics.

14. TEMPORAL MODALITIES AMONG THE SCHOOLMEN

The Latin medievals appear to have taken the theory of temporal modalities over from the Arabs to at any rate a modest extent. In Albert the Great, for example, we find a return to the temporalized modalities in the manner of the Stoics. According to him, modal propositions have a *consignificatio temporis*: a reference to the future is inherent in the modalities *possible* and *contingens*, while the modalities *necessarium* and *impossibile* involve an omnitemporal thesis. The possible is that which will be at some future time; the contingent is that which is, but will at some future time not be; [39] the necessary is that which will be always, the impossible never.[40] St. Albert explicitly polemicizes against those who, while granting that the contingent involves reference to the future, deny that the possible

---

[39] Or, of course, the negative counterpart of this, viz. that which is not, but will at some future time be. Cf. Boethius' characterization of future contingent propositions as *propositiones, quae cum non sint, eas tamen in futurum evenire possibile est.* This mode of contingency is also present in Albert under the name of *contingens futurum*, and was to give rise to ramified disputes among his successors. See P. Boehner, The " *Tractatus de praedestinatione et de praescientia Dei et de futuribus contingentibus* " *of William of Ockham* (St. Bonaventure, New York, 1945; Franciscan Institute Publications, No. 2) and L. Baudry, *La Querelle des futurs contingents (Louvain 1465–1475)* (Paris, 1950; Etudes de philosophie médiévale, fasc. XXXVIII).

[40] *Quatuor enim primi illorum modorum (sc. possibile, contingens, necessarium et impossibile) compositionem (quae consignificat tempus) ampliant extra tempus praesens. Possibile enim et contingens ampliant praesens ad futurum, et ad esse, et ad non esse: quia contingens est futurum, et potest esse et non esse. Necessarium autem et impossibile ampliant compositionem ad omne tempus: quia necessarium et impossibile ponunt compositionem in omne tempus: et ideo illi sunt modi speciales facientes totam enuntiationem modalem, necessarium simpliciter omni tempore inesse, et impossibile simpliciter nunquam inesse.* (*Commentaria in libro II, Perihermeneias*, tract II, cap. 1; ed. A. Borgnet, vol. I [Paris, 1890], p. 440a, b.) On the theory of the temporal " ampliation " of the terms of categorical propositions widely current among the Medieval schoolmen see E. A. Moody, *Truth and Consequence in Medieval Logic* (Amsterdam, 1953).

does. The possible was already possible prior to its actualization, and so its qualification as possible at this prior juncture must derive from an inherent reference to the future.[41]

In Pseudo-Scotus we find a distinction between four types of temporalized " necessity " (*conditionale* = conditional, *quando* = as-long-as, *ut nunc* = as-of-now, and *pro semper* = for all times).[42] I would conjecture a correspondence with the cognate Arabic ideas along something like the following lines:

Pseudo Scotus	*Construction*	*al-Qazwini*
1. *quando*	$(A/\Box/E![A])$	absolute necessary
2. *pro semper*	$(A/\forall t/E![A])$	absolute perpetual
3. *conditionale*	$(A/\Box/C[A])$	general conditional
4. *ut nunc* [43]	$(A/\exists t/E![A])$	general absolute

If this conjecture—or anything like it—is correct, temporalized modalities also found made their way pretty well intact into the Latin scholastics. While this development could have been mediated (or perhaps only strengthened) through Arabic materials, it could also have been indigenous to a purely Latin tradition. Signs of this are already to be found in Boethius:

> *Ea vero quae ex necessitate aliquid inesse designat tribus dicitur modis; uno quidem quo ei similis est propositioni quae inesse significat . . . alia vero necessitatis significatio est, cum hoc modo proponimus " hominem necesse est cor habere, dum est atque vivit " . . . alia vero necessitatis significatio est universalis et propria quo absolute praedicat necessitatem . . . possibile autem idem tribus dicitur modis; aut enim quod est, possibile esse dicitur . . . aut quod omni tempore contingere potest, cum ea res permanet cui aliquid contingere posse proponitur . . . item possibile est quod absolute omni tempore contingere potest. . . . ex his igitur apparet alias propositiones esse inesse significantes alias necessarias alias contingentes atque possibiles, quarum necessariarum contingentiumque cum sit trina partitio, singulae ex iisdem partionibus ad eas quae inesse significant referentur; restant igitur duae necessariae et duae contingentes*

---

[41] *Non est verum quod quidam dicunt, quod contingens differat a possibili in hoc, quod contingens dicat extensionem temporis in futurum, et possibile non dicat illud: possibile enim ante actum acceptum extenditur in futurum.* (*Ibid.*, tract II, cap. 6; Borgnet, vol. I, p. 452a, b.)

[42] I. M. Bocheński, o.p., *Notes historiques sur les propositions modales* (Quebec, 1951), p. 7.

[43] We here construe " *nunc* " not as *the now* (that is, the now-of-the-present), but as *a now* (that is, some—i.e., *any*—instant). This dual interpretation is standard in the medievals.

quae cum ea quae inesse significat enumeratae quinque omnes propositionum faciunt differentias; omnium vero harum propositionum aliae sunt affirmativae aliae negativae.[44]

Cognate distinctions are also drawn elsewhere. For example, in St. Thomas Aquinas and other medieval scholastics we find a distinction—akin to the modern distinction between logical and physical necessity—between those relationships which are perpetual and (in a sense) necessary: (1) by an eternity that is *a parte ante*, or (2) by an eternity that is *a parte post*. Truths of the former class are necessary by a necessity that turns wholly on the nature of the essences involved—as men are eternally rational and equiangular triangles eternally equilateral. Truths of the second class are necessary by a necessity that devolves from the *au fond* contingent arrangements of this world—as men are eternally mortal, or the northern latitudes eternally cold.[45] Traces of an interest in such temporal modalities are to be found as late as William of Ockham.[46]

15. Conclusion

We have seen that ideas of temporalized modality originating in ancient Greece were carried forward and elaborated with a high degree of sophistication by Arabic logicians of the middle ages. The intricacy of the modal notions at issue was such that, in the context of complex interrelationships—and especially in the modal syllogistic —errors tended to creep in. Nevertheless, the basic ideas were clear and the guiding intuitions of their elaboration straightforwardly intelligible. It is, I believe, safe to say that—barring possible new findings from the side of medieval Latin scholasticism—the logical theory of temporal concepts was carried to a higher point in Arabic logic than at any subsequent juncture prior to our own times.

---

[44] Quoted from C. Prantl, *Geschichte der Logik im Abendlande*, vol. I (Leipzig, 1855; photoreprinted, Graz, 1955), p. 703, no. 150.

[45] See Guy Jalbert, *op. cit.*, pp. 41, 119–120, 137–138, 141–143. This work is primarily concerned with possible and necessary *existents*. A detailed treatment of such existents, primarily in Avicenna, but with some comparisons and contrasts in St. Thomas, can be found in Gerard Smith, "Avicenna and the Possibles," *The New Scholasticism*, vol. 17 (1943) 340–357.

[46] *Summa logicae* (ed. P. Boehner), pt. I, ch. 73, lines 16–49; pt. II, ch's 7, 19–22; pt. III, div. i, ch's 17–19.

VIII

IBN AL-'ASSĀL'S DISCOURSE ON LOGIC

A. Introduction

Al-Mu'taman abū Isḥāq ibn al-'Assāl flourished in Cairo in the first half of the 13th century. He came of an important family of scholars, and two of his older stepbrothers, Ṣafī and Hibat Allāh, were writers of considerable importance.[1] Ibn al-'Assāl wrote extensively on philological, philosophical, and especially on theological subjects.

In 1904, Father P. C. Eddé (Khalīl Iddih), S.J., published in the Lebanese periodical *Al-Mashriq*[2] an edition of Ibn al-'Assāl's " Discourse on Logic " (*Maqālah fī 'l-manṭiq*) extracted from this author's philosophico-theological Summa " The Roots of Religion " (*Uṣūl al-dīn*).[3] (Father Eddé transcribed the treatise from a manuscript in his possession as part of his superb collection of Arabic manuscripts.) This publication gave Ibn al-'Assāl's tract the distinction of being among the earliest of the few Arabic logic-texts that have—even at the present day—seen the light of print in the original.

The second part of this paper will present an annotated translation of Ibn al-'Assāl's discourse. Before turning to this, a few preliminary observations are in order.

Ibn al-'Assāl's discourse is by no means a short manual of logic, of the sort so popular among the Arabs. It ignores vast reaches of the

---

[1] See Alexis Mallon, " Ibn al-Assāl: Les trois écrivains de ce nom," *Journal Asiatique*, X série, vol. 6 (1903), pp. 509–529. And cf. also N. Rescher, *The Development of Arabic Logic* (Pittsburgh, 1964), pp. 193–194.

[2] Vol. 7 (1904), pp. 811–819 and 1072–1078; cf. vol. 9 (1906), p. 757.

[3] Eddé at first wrongly attributed this work to the brother, Hibat Allāh. Brockelmann, GAL, Supplementband I, p. 368. The discourse is given in the second chapter (*faṣl*) of the first part (*maqālah*).

subject altogether (e.g., the survey of the valid moods of the cate-gorical syllogism), and concentrates entirely on four topics:
(1) the classification of terms
(2) the classification of propositions
(3) the modes of modality (with special reference to the contradiction of modal propositions)
(4) the classification of syllogisms

The treatment of this material is not original, but follows the tracks of Avicenna and his school. All the same, it is a useful summary of what is essentially the standard Arabic logicians' way of looking at these matters. Item (3) is of particular interest for it supplements in significant respects the discussion of the theory of modality in the " Sun Epistle " (*Al-Risālah al-shamsiyyah*) of Al-Qazwīnī al-Kātibī, one of the few Arabic treatises dealing with these matters that has been printed and studied to the present day.[4] The modal machinery that is presented is of a highly intricate constitution. Modal pro-positions are classed into thirteen different sorts:

1. General Possible
2. Special Possible
3. General Absolute
4. Perpetual
5. General Conventional
6. Special Conventional
7. Non-perpetual Existential
8. Absolute Necessary
9. General Conditional
10. Special Conditional
11. Temporal
12. Spread
13. Non-necessary Existential

These modal distinctions, which are in fact drawn on the basis of complex chronological considerations, are not at all adequately explained in our text.[5] Despite this deficiency, our text does, in the context of others, help to illuminate the nature of these modalities, particularly as concerns the manner of their negation (i.e., contra-diction). In particular, the " Sun Epistle " deals with the negation of the compound modalities in the briefest way, whereas our text enters into more extensive detail, and gives examples.

The nature of the temporal modalities can be made clearer with the help of the following symbolism. $A, B, C, \ldots$ are to be variables standing for categorical propositions. The contradictory of a

---

[4] See the preceding chapter as well as N. Rescher, *Temporal Modalities in Arabic Logic* (Dordrecht, 1966) and also Aloys Sprenger, *Dictionary of the Technical Terms Used in the Sciences of the Musulmans*, Pt. 2; Calcutta, 1962; Appendix I on " The Logic of the Arabians."

[5] For a full explanation, drawing upon various other sources, see the preceding chapter.

proposition A will be symbolized as $\sim A$. $[A]$ will represent the subject of the proposition A, and $E![A]$ is to mean that the subject of A exists, i.e., that it is actually exemplified. (It should be noted that because $[A] = [\sim A]$, $E![A]$ will mean the same as $E![\sim A]$.) $C[A]$ will mean that the subject of A satisfies the condition C. In addition to the quantity and the quality of the categorical proposition A, the modal proposition will bear one of the modal qualifiers, necessary, not necessary, perpetual, or not perpetual.

There are four basic modal relationships, symbolized as follows, out of which the thirteen modal propositions are then constructed. These four are:

1. $(A/\Box/B)$ meaning " A is necessarily true whenever B is true."
2. $(A/\forall t/B)$ meaning " A is true whenever B is true."
3. $(A/\exists t/B)$ meaning " A is true at some time that B is true."
4. $(A/\Diamond/B)$ meaning " A is possible at some time that B is true."

For a fuller and more precise explication of the ideas at issue Sect. 5 of the preceding chapter may be consulted.

The six simple and seven compound modal propositions can then be presented according to the following table:

Name	Construction
1. Absolute necessary	$(A/\Box/E![A])$
2. Absolute perpetual	$(A/\forall t/E![A])$
3. General conditional	$(A/\Box/C[A])$
4. General conventional	$(A/\forall t/C[A])$
5. General absolute	$(A/\exists t/E![A])$
6. General possible	$(A/\Diamond/E![A])$
7. Special conditional (3 & $\sim$5)	$(A/\Box/C[A])$ & $(\sim A/\exists t/E![\sim A])$
8. Special conventional (4 & $\sim$5)	$(A/\forall t/C[A])$ & $(\sim A/\exists t/E![\sim A])$
9. Non-necessary existential (5 & $\sim$6)	$(A/\exists t/E![A])$ & $(\sim A/\Diamond/E![\sim A])$
10. Non-perpetual existential (5 & $\sim$5)	$(A/\exists t/E![A])$ & $(\sim A/\exists t/E![\sim A])$
11. Temporal (3 & $\sim$5)	$(A/\Box/T[A])$ & $(\sim A/\exists t/E![\sim A])$
12. Spread (3 & $\sim$5)	$(A/\Box/S[A])$ & $(\sim A/\exists t/E![\sim A])$
13. Special possible (6 & $\sim$6)	$(A/\Diamond/E![A])$ & $(\sim A/\Diamond/E![\sim A])$ [6]

[6] The intrinsic completeness of this enumeration was shown in Sect. 7 of the preceding chapter.

By way of illustration, if A is the categorical proposition " All fire is hot," the Absolute Perpetual modal proposition would read " When there is fire, then it is necessarily hot." The Non-necessary Existential proposition would read " When there is fire it is sometimes hot and (but) it is possible that it not be hot." If A is the categorical proposition " Some men are not wise " then the Absolute Perpetual is " When there are men, then there are always some who are not wise," and the Special Possible is " When there are men, then possibly some of them are not wise and (but) possibly all are wise."

The contradictory of a simple modal proposition is obtained by interchanging A and $\sim A$, $\square$ and $\Diamond$, $\forall t$ and $\exists t$, wherever they occur, and replacing $C[A]$ in the original by $E![A]$ in the negation. Thus the negation of the General Absolute is $(\sim A/\forall t/E![\sim A])$, that is, an Absolute Perpetual proposition, and the negation of a General Conditional is $(\sim A/\Diamond/E![\sim A])$, that is, a General Possible proposition.

The negation of a compound proposition is obtained by negating each of the constituent conjuncts, and putting them into a disjunction. Thus the negation of the Special Possible is a disjunction of two Necessary Absolutes, i.e., $(\sim A/\square/E![A])$ v $(A/\square/E![A])$. The negation of the Special Conditional is the disjunction of a General Possible and an Absolute Perpetual, i.e., $(\sim A/\Diamond/E![\sim A])$ v $(A/\forall t/E![A])$. (It should be noted that these rules for the formation of contradictories correspond to negation in standard quantification theory except for the treatment of the special conditions C, S, T.) The situation as regarding the contradiction of the chronologized modal propositions is set out in detail in Tables I and II.

Table I

Contradictories of Simple Modal Propositions

	Original		Contradictory	
Name	*Form*	*Form*		*Name*
1. Absolute necessary	$(A/\square/E![A])$	$(\sim A/\Diamond/E![\sim A])$		General possible
2. (Absolute) perpetual	$(A/\forall t/E![A])$	$(\sim A/\exists t/E![\sim A])$		General absolute

	Original		Contradictory	
Name	*Form*	*Form*		*Name*
3. General				General
conditional	$(A/\Box/C[A])$	$(\sim A/\Diamond/E![\sim A])$		possible *
4. General				General
conventional	$(A/\forall t/C[A])$	$(\sim A/\exists t/E![\sim A])$		absolute *
5. General				(Absolute)
absolute	$(A/\exists t/E![A])$	$(\sim A/\forall t/E![\sim A])$		perpetual
6. General				Absolute
possible	$(A/\Diamond/E![A])$	$(\sim A/\Box/E![\sim A])$		necessary

* In the formation of contradictories, the special condition C is treated simply as the existence-condition $E!$.

Table II

Contradictories of Compound Modal Propositions

Name	*Form*	*Form of Contradictory*
	Conjunction of	Disjunction of
7. Special	Gen. Cond. and Gen. Abs.	Gen. Poss. or Abs. Perp.*
conditional	$(A/\Box/C[A])$ &	$(\sim A/\Diamond/E![\sim A])$ v
	$(\sim A/\exists t/E![\sim A])$	$(A/\forall t/E![\sim A])$
8. Special con-	Gen. Conv. and Gen. Abs.	Gen. Abs. or Abs. Perp.*
ventional	$(A/\forall t/C[A])$ &	$(\sim A/\exists t/E![\sim A])$ v
	$(\sim A/\exists t/E![\sim A])$	$(A/\forall t/E![A])$
9. Non-necessary	Gen. Abs. and Gen. Poss.	Abs. Perp. or Nec. Abs.
existential	$(A/\exists t/E![A])$ &	$(\sim A/\forall t/E![\sim A])$ v
	$(\sim A/\Diamond/E![\sim A])$	$(A/\Box/E![A])$
10. Non-perpetual	Gen. Abs. and Gen. Abs.	Abs. Perp. or Abs. Perp.
existential	$(A/\exists t/E![A])$ &	$(\sim A/\forall t/E![\sim A])$ v
	$(\sim A/\exists t/E![\sim A])$	$(A/\forall t/E![A])$
11. Temporal	Gen. Cond. and Gen. Abs.	Gen. Poss. or Abs. Perp.
	$(A/\Box/T(A))$ &	$(\sim A/\Diamond/E![\sim A])$ v
	$(\sim A/\exists t/E!\sim[A])$	$(A/\forall t/E![A])$
12. Spread	Gen. Cond. and Gen. Abs.	Gen. Poss. or Abs. Perp.*
	$(A/\Box/S(A))$ &	$(\sim A/\Diamond/E![\sim A])$ v
	$(\sim A/\exists t/E![\sim A])$	$(A/\forall t/E![A])$
13. Special	Gen. Poss. and Gen. Poss.	Nec. Abs. or Nec. Abs.
possible	$(A/\Diamond/E![A])$ &	$(\sim A/\Box/E![\sim A])$ v
	$(\sim A/\Diamond/E!\sim[A])$	$(A/\Box/E![A])$

* In the formation of contradictories, the special conditions C, T, and S are treated simply as the existence-condition $E!$.

A few words regarding the mechanics of the translation are in order. The translation is very literal—as is necessary to render a text of this sort useful for scholarly purposes. The correspondence with the Arabic text (as printed in Father Eddé's transcription) is indicated on a line-by-line basis. (For grammatical reasons this cannot but be occasionally imperfect.) The division of the translation into paragraphs is, in general, without textual warrant and dictated by the sense of the discussion alone. The use in the translation of enumerations and labeled lists is entirely of our devising.[7]

B. Translation of Ibn al-'Assāl's Discourse

[712: 25]   *Words*

/26/ A useful word is either (1) considered in relation to the whole of what is named, such as *man* in relation to /27/ *rational* [*animal*], which is the indication by *equivalence*, or (2) a part of what is named insofar as it is a part, like *man* /28/ [in relation] to *rational* or *animal* by itself, which is the indication by *inclusion*, or (3) something external but necessary which is transferred to it /29/ from what is named, like *lion* [in relation] to *courage* or *donkey* [in relation] to *laziness*, which is the indication [713: 1] by *connection*.

The indication of equivalence is the valid mode, and the other two are figuration [or: *metaphorical*]. The [indication by] inclusion is called " applying the name /2/ of the whole to the part," and the indication by connection [is called] " applying the name of the connected to its connectee."

/3/ The indication by equivalence [is such that] either (1) a part of it indicates a part of the whole when it is a part of it, /4/ such as *the house of Zayd* and *Amr the boy*, and this is the *compound*, or (2) it does not indicate [in this way], and this is the *singular*. And it [may] either (i) be defined in [a single] meaning /5/ with different words like *felix leo* and *lion*, or *wine* and *vinous liquor*, and these are synonyms; or (ii) be defined in [a single] word that differs /6/ in meaning

[7] I am grateful to Mr. Sesostris M. Khalil for some help with the translation. Also, I wish to thank Virginia (Mrs. Peder) Hong for assistance in compiling and checking some of the data presented in the Introduction.

[both] in definition and in fact—such as *the eye* of vision and *the eye* of
a needle ⁸ or as *the buyer* who accepts an agreement of sale, /7/ and
the star (Jupiter) ⁹ which the astrologers regard as bearing good
luck—and these are the *equivocal names* which name a group of
[different] things in relation /8/ to each one of its [different]
meanings. It may also (*a*) be defined by words that differ in
meaning not in definition and in fact, but in number only— /9/ such
as *man* in relation to each individual and *animal* in relation to each
particular one, and *horse* in relation to each of its units—and
/10/ these are the *common names*, i.e., those whose definition is
uniform in its meaning. Or (*b*) there is a plurality in [both] the word
and the meaning together, and these are /11/ the *differentiated names*,
alike whether (*a*) they indicate an essence, like *winter* and *earth*, or
(*β*) whether one indicates an essence /12/ and the other an accident
such as *sword* and *the sharp*, or (*γ*) a conjunction of an essence and an
accident, such as *the Indian* (*sword*), which indicates /13/ the essence
of the sword together with its feature of stemming from India, or
(*δ*) an accident of an accident, such as *the eloquent speaker*.

* * *

/14/ The singular ¹⁰ either (1) is not independent because
something [must be] reported of it, and this is the particle,¹¹ or (2) it
is independent because nothing [must be] reported of it, and this
either /15/ (i) indicates a certain determinate time for its existence
with its characteristics, and these are the forms which characterize
the infinitives in conjugation /16/ such as *to strike, to have struck*, and
this is *the verb* or (ii) it does not indicate [a certain determinate time]
and this is *the noun*. It (i.e., a noun) either (*a*) prevents the mind
from picturing the meaning /17/ in it of something shared in
common [by many], such as *Zayd* and *Amr*, and this is *the proper
name*, both particular and individual in meaning, or (*b*) it does not
prevent [such depiction], /18/ and this is the universal, and is

⁸ Arabic has an expression " eye of a fountain," and this is used here.
⁹ Also called " the buyer " in Arabic.
¹⁰ Cf. case (2) of line 4 above.
¹¹ *Al-adāt*, used by the Arab grammarians for that which is neither a noun nor
a verb.

called *the general name.* And this is either (α) a complete " whatness," or (β) is included in the " whatness," and /19/ is something such that the " whatness " does not exist without its existence and is destroyed with its destruction, both in the external world [12] and in the mind together; and this is called /20/ *essential* to that " whatness." Or (γ) it is external to it (i.e., the " whatness "), and this is what is not of this [previous] sort, and is called accidental to it (i.e., that " whatness ").

*   *   *

/21/ That which is included in the " whatness " [13] is either:

(1) predicated of many actually different things in answer to the question " What is it? ", /22/ and this is the totality of the part shared among them [all]—such as *substance* and *matter* and *ensouled body* and *animal*—and this is /23/ *the genus,* because it is a universal predicated of many actually different things in answer to the question " What is it? " This [i.e., the genus] is of four /24/ kinds. [14]

Or (2) it is predicated of many things different in number in answer to [the question] " What kind (species) is it? "; and this is the totality of the part [714: 1] distinctive of it—such as reasoning in relation to animals [15]—because it is a universal predicated of many things different in number in answer to [the question] /2/ " What kind (species) is it? " This is [something such that] it is not possible that it be nonexistent, because nonexistence is not possibly a part of /3/ an existent. And it is not necessary that there be a cause [of it] through the existence of a cause of the species of material-body (i.e., a material cause), because *growing body* is the genus of [both] *plant* /4/ and *animal,* and both of them are distinguished from the others by a power existing in this [growing] body. And the existence of the [particular] thing /5/ requires it (the universal), so that it is impossible that it (the thing) should be its (the universal's) cause. The division is a divider of the genus governing over the species: whenever /6/ the species is divided the genus is [also] divided, but not conversely.

---

[12] Literally: *in the exterior.*

[13] Cf. the immediately preceding case (β). But the matter is resumed at 714: 15–16 below.

[14] They are, surprisingly, not enumerated here.

[15] That is, when man is defined *per genus et differentiam* as " the rational animal."

/7/ The principle of whatness [16] is either (1) predicated of many things different in number only in answer to /8/ [the question] " What is it? " like *man* in relation to its [exemplifying] individuals.[17] This is the true species, because it is a universal predicated /9/ of many things different in number [only] in answer to [the question] " What is it? " Or (2) it is [used as] the subject of some genus which is above it, /10/ and is divided off from it in meaning, so that this [genus] is said of it, and also others of this genus, in answer to [the question] " What is it? " as man is /11/ in relation to the animals.[18] This [second] factor is the relative (or: *supplementary*) species.

This has four kinds also, since there will either (i) /12/ be a species above it, but not a species under it, e.g., *horse*, and this is the *ultimate* [i.e., *infimum*] *species* and is [also] called " the species of species " [i.e., *the species* in the strictest sense]. Or (ii) /13/ the reverse [i.e., with a species below it but none above], and this is the *highest* (or: *supreme*) *species*. Or (iii) there is a species above it and a species below it, e.g., *animal* or *sleeping* [*living*] *body* (?), /14/ and this is *the intermediate species*. Or (iv) there is not a species above it nor a species below it, e.g., *angel*, and this is *the isolated species*. This /15/ is also to be said about the kinds of genera,[19] except that the highest is then *substance* " the genus of genera," [20] which is the /16/ ultimate [i.e., *supreme*] genus. [An example of] the isolated genus is *intellect* since it is not a genus of *substance*.

/17/ As regards what is separated from " whatness," [21] this either: (1) Is necessary to it and pertains to [all of] a single species as *the power of laughter* /18/ in relation to man, and this is the *specific* [*accident*].[22] Or (2) [it pertains] to more than one species, as *the moving* or *the existing* /19/ [obtain] in relation to many species, and this is the *general accident*. Or (3) it is not necessary to it (i.e., to the

---

[16] See item (*a*) at 713: 18–20 above.
[17] Q: What is this? A: *This* is a *man*. Here we have the case of species and individual instance in answer to a *what-is-it?* question.
[18] Q: What is man? A: *Man* is an *animal*. Here we have the case of species and genus in answer to a *what-is-it?* question.
[19] Cf. 713: 23–24 above.
[20] That is, the highest genus in *the genus* in the strictest sense, unlike the case of species, where the lowest is *the species* in the strictest sense.
[21] Cf. item (*γ*) at 713: 20 above.
[22] Or: *characteristic accident*.

STUDIES IN ARABIC PHILOSOPHY

species), and this is the *differential accident*, which /20/ is also called a *specific* [*accident*] when it pertains to one species only and a *general accident* when it is found in more than a /21/ single species. It may be *ephemeral* [23] like the blush of shyness or the blanching of fear, or /22/ *perduring* [24] like old age and youth.

* * *

/23/ As to the compound,[25] it is either (1) restricted [26] like *the rational animal* in the definition of man—or (2) it is propositional, and this is [815: 1] *the* [*complete*] *judgment*, or (3) it is neither restricted nor propositional; and this [third] is either (i) used to ask for something—the main use—or (ii) it is not so used. Now if /2/ it is the first (i.e., asks for something) then the sought-for [reply] is either (*a*) the " whatness " (essence, *māhiyyah*) things, and this is *the question* (proper), or (*b*) it is an act arising from someone addressed, /3/ and this [if issued] with superiority is an *order*, and [if issued] with subordination is a *plea* [or: *a begging*], and [if issued] with equality is a *request*. This makes clear the difference between /4/ the statement " What is the husband? " on the one hand and " Inform me: what is the delineation (or: *definition*) of the husband? " on the other—because the sought-for [reply] of the first [question] is the " whatness " /5/ of the husband, but that of the second is knowledge of the " whatness " of this " whatness." But if it is the second (i.e., does not ask for something),[27] then it is a *warning* (or: *counsel*), whose stages are *the wish* /6/ and *the request* and *the oath* and *the imprecation*.

* * *

As for the definition, it is either (1) by genus and difference, as in the statement " Man /7/ is a rational animal," which is the *complete* (or: *perfect*) *definition*; or (2) it is by difference alone as in the statement " Man is the rational " which is /8/ the *incomplete* (or: *imperfect*) *definition*; or (3) it is by genus and a differentiating-characteristic, as in the statement " Man is the laughing animal "

---

[23] Literally: *swift to vanish.*
[24] Literally: *slow to vanish.*
[25] See 713: 4 above.
[26] That is, limited or incomplete.
[27] That is, the second alternative of line 1 above.

which is the *complete* (or: *perfect*) *description*; /9/ or (4) it is by a differentiating-characteristic alone, like the statement " Man is the laughing," which is the *incomplete* (or: *imperfect*) *description*.

/10/ *The Proposition*

/11/ As to the *proposition*, it is a statement that admits either truth or falsity, like the statement " A material-body is movable " that is, " A material-body /12/ has motion "—which is called a *derivative predicate*—or like the statement " The movable is a material-body," that is " That which has motion is a material-body " /13/—which is called an *agreeing predicate*.

The judgment in a proposition is either (1) decisive as we have illustrated, and thus is the *categorical* [proposition], or /14/ (2) it is connected with a condition, and thus is the *conditional*. Then this connection is either (*a*) a necessary connection, which is conjoined as in the statement /15/ " Whenever the sun is risen, then day exists," or (*b*) it is a contradictory connection which is conjoined as in the statement " Every number is either /16/ even or odd."

As to the categorical proposition, it must have a *subject*, which is that which is judged about, and a *predicate*, which is /17/ that which is judged about it. These are the *described* and the *description* in the technical terminology of kalām, and the *grammatical-subject* and the *grammatical-predicate* in grammar.

It is not /18/ a [necessary] condition for the existence of a thing as subject that its existence is an actual fact at the time that it exists as subject, but it suffices for its existence [816: 1] as subject that it simply exists in general, indifferently in the past or the present or the future.

/2/ If the subject is particular, the proposition is called *special*, like the sentences " Zayd is a clerk," " Zayd is not a clerk." /3/ And if it (the subject) is universal, then it (i.e., the proposition) is either (1) restricted by a quantity-indicator—" all " or " some " or " nothing " or " not one " or " not /4/ all " or " not some " or " some not." This is the expression which indicates the quantity of the collectivity of which the judgment is affirmed. /5/ The thus-enclosed proposition is called restricted. Or (2) it (i.e., the proposition) is not restricted by a quantity-indicator, be it affirmative

/6/ or negative. It is then called an " indeterminate " [literally: *neglected*] proposition, as for example the statements " Man is a creature-that-laughs," " Man is not a creature-that-laughs." These statements are /7/ particulars in their force, because of their agreement [28] in truth with the truth of the particular rather than the universal.

* * *

The (quantitatively) enclosed proposition divides into /8/ (1) the *universal*, which is that restricted by the quantity-indicator " all " or " no " or " not a single "; and this is [also] called *general*; and (2) the *particular*, which is that restricted /9/ by the quantity-indicator " some " or " not every " and it is [also] called *special*. Then both the universal and the particular are divided into /10/ (*a*) the *affirmative*, in which one judges one thing to hold positively (or: *determinately*) about another thing—be they existents or nonexistents or one of them /11/ an existent and the other a nonexistent; and it is [also] called positive (or: *determinate*); and into (*b*) the *negative*, in which one judges that one thing does not hold positively /12/ of another thing—as we explained in the commentary [29]—and it is [also] called a *denial*.

Thus there are four [types of] restricted [propositions], as follows: " Every man /13/ is an animal," " Some animal is a man," " No man is a horse," and " Some animal is not a horse " /14/ or [equivalently] " Not every animal is a horse," since there is no distance between them in meaning.

* * *

Then both the affirmative and the negative /15/ divide into (1) the *corresponding*, which is that in which a negative particle is put as part of the predicate or the subject or /16/ both together—as in the statement " Everything that is not-alive is inert, and everything inert is not-endowed-with-knowledge, so everything that is not-/17/ alive is not-endowed-with-knowledge [30]—and (2) the *con-*

[28] I suppose the reading *w-f-q* for *w-q-f* of the printed text.
[29] It is not clear which commentary is at issue.
[30] The salient feature of this otherwise straightforward *AAA-1* (*Barbara*) syllogism is its use of the terms " not-alive " and " not-endowed-with-knowledge " which contain the negative particle " not."

sequential, and (3) the *simple* which are not of this sort: the consequential pertains /18/ to the affirmative and the simple to the negative. The priority belongs to the precedence of the negative particle upon the linkage if /19/ the proposition is a triple, but if it is a double then this would be either arbitrary (literally: *by wish or by intention*) or conventional.[31]

/20/ *On the Modality of Propositions*

/21/ The relationship of predicates to subjects has a quality, be the relationship affirmative or negative, [817: 1] and this quality is called the *modality* of the proposition. These are six [in number] because they are [divided] either in power (potentiality), and this is /2/ the *special possible,* or in fact (actuality), and this is the *general absolute.* Then that in fact (i.e., the actual or existential) is either by perpetuity, and this is the *perpetual,* or it is not /3/ by perpetuity, and this is the *non-perpetual [existential].* Then the perpetual is either by necessity, and this is the *absolute necessary,* or it is not [818: 1] by necessity, and this is the *non-necessary [existential].*[32]

These six modalities are judged about [all] assertions. It is not possible /2/ for any proposition to be lacking in them as regards the matter itself, although they may not be mentioned [explicitly], so that they are not indicated in words. /3/ But it is impossible for none of these modalities to qualify the matter itself. */6/ If it (a proposition) is not modalized in /7/ words and is not bounded by any [modal] bound (or: *limit*) at all, then one must seek to determine what its modality is. And if it is modalized /8/ in words in one of the modalities we have mentioned, then either it will be:* [33]

/4/ (1) The *general possible* which is applicable to all of the propositions that are bound by a general possibility in which one judges /5/ by removing the necessary from the side (or: *part*) that is

[31] The exact import of this paragraph is quite unclear.

[32] This classification is apparently badly garbled. It makes little sense in the light of the ensuing discussion. Perhaps the author intended to list the six basic modes of modality. Cf. Sect. 6 of ch. VII above. If so, however, his list is for the most part incorrect. It is possible that the intention is to list all of the modalities not involving a special condition (C, T, or S). In this case the list is correct and complete except for the omission of the *general possible.*

[33] We transpose the two sentences enclosed by asterisks from lines 6–8 to make smoother sense of the discussion.

opposite to it—as in the statement: " Every fire is hot by a general possibility and everything /6/ hot burns by a general possibility, so therefore every fire burns by a general possibility." [34] Or

/8/ (2) It is indicated by a special possibility, and this /9/ is the *special possible*, i.e., the one (modal proposition) that judges by removing necessity from the sides (or: *parts*) both of the existent and the nonexistent, /10/ alike whether it (the proposition) be universal or particular, affirmative or negative,—as in the statements " All gold is meltable by a special possibility," /11/ and " All gold is solidifiable by a special possibility."

Or (3) it is modalized by a *general absolute*, and this is either:

(4) In relation to the duration /12/ of the essence of the subject, and this is the *perpetual* in which one judges about the duration of the continuation of the predicate in the subject, or its denial, /13/ in relation to the duration of the essence of the subject [35]—as in the statement: " Perpetually every material-body is composite, and Perpetually no necessary /14/ existent is composite, so consequently, Perpetually no material-body is a necessary existent." [36]

Or in relation to the duration of the characterization of the subject [by the predicate], /15/ either (5) absolutely, and this is the *general conventional* proposition, that is, one in which one judges regarding duration of the continuation of the predicate in the subject, /16/ or its denial, in relation to the duration of the continuation of the characterization of the subject [by the predicate] [37]—as in the statement: " Every animal is a sensitive-being as long as it is an animal, and No /17/ animal is inert [as long as it is an animal], so consequently Some sensitive-being is not inert as long as it is a sensitive-being." [38]

[34] This is an *AAA-1* (*Barbara*) syllogism, with both premisses and conclusion uniformly modalized in the modality of the general possible.

[35] That is, so long as the essence of the subject exists. An example would be: " *Perpetually*: Every physician is rational."

[36] This is an *EAE-2* (*Cesare*) syllogism with both premisses and conclusion uniformly modalized in the mode of perpetuity.

[37] So long as the description of the subject exists (i.e., pertains to it). An example would be: " *Perpetually*: Every physician can diagnose diseases." (Contrast with this example that of n. 35.)

[38] This is an *EAO-3* (*Felapton*) syllogism, with both premisses and conclusion uniformly modalized in the mode of limited perpetuity characteristic of the general conventional proposition.

Or (6) it is bound (or: *limited*) /18/ by the bound (or: *limit*) of non-perpetuity, and this is the *special conventional* [proposition], that is, one in which one judges regarding the duration of the continuation of the predicate in the subject, or /19/ its denial, that it is non-perpetual in relation to the duration of the essence of the subject, but [that it *is* perpetual] in relation to the duration of a characteristic of the subject—as in the statement: " No /20/ intoxicant is grapes, not perpetually but as long as it is an intoxicant, and All wine is an intoxicant, not perpetually but as long as it is /21/ wine, so consequently No grapes are wine, not perpetually but as long as they are grapes." [39]

Or (7) it is modalized by the modality of the non-perpetual, and this is /22/ the *non-perpetual existential*, i.e., the one [modal proposition] in which one judges about the continuation of the predicate in the subject, or its denial, as being [actual but] non-perpetual— /23/ as in the statement " Some persons are laughers, actually but not perpetually, and No laughers are sleepers, actually but not perpetually, /24/ so consequently Some persons are not sleepers, [actually but] not perpetually." [40]

Or it is modalized by the modality of the necessary, and this either (8) in relation to the duration of the essence /25/ of the subject as being in perpetuity, and this is the *absolute necessary* [proposition], i.e., that in which one judges about the necessary duration of the continuation /26/ of the predicate in the subject, or its denial, in relation to the essence of the subject [itself]—as in the statement " By necessity every corporeal-substance is possible, and [819: 1] By necessity, nothing possible is excluded so necessarily No corporeal-substance is excluded." [41]

Or in relation to /2/ the duration of a characteristic of the subject, either (9) absolutely—as in the general conventional—and this is the *general conditional* [proposition], i.e., the one in which one judges

[39] This an *AEE*-4 (*Camenes*) syllogism, with both premises and conclusion uniformly modalized in the temporally restricted mode characteristic of the special conventional proposition.
[40] This is an *EIO*-1 (*Ferio*) syllogism, with both premises and conclusion uniformly modalized in the mode of (non-perpetual) actuality characteristic of the non-perpetual existential proposition.
[41] This is an *EAE*-1 (*Celarent*) syllogism, with both premises and conclusion uniformly modalized in the mode of absolute necessity.

/3/ about the necessary duration of the continuation of the predicate [in the subject], or its denial, in relation to the duration of a description of the subject—as in the statements: " /4/ By necessity, every writer moves as long as he is writing, and By necessity, nothing that moves is at rest while it is /5/ moving,[42] writing, [so consequently, By necessity, No writer is at rest as long as he is writing]."[43]

Or (10) bound (or: *limited*) by the bound (or: *limit*) of the nonperpetual—as in the special conventional—and this is the *special conditional*, i.e., the one in which one judges /6/ about the necessary duration of the continuation of the predicate in the subject, or its denial, as being perpetual not in relation to the duration of the essence /7/ of the subject, but in relation to the duration of a characteristic of the subject—as in the statement: " By necessity, no waking-creature is sleeping, not /8/ perpetually but as long as it is waking, and By necessity, every asleep-creature is sleeping, not perpetually but while it is asleep, /9/ so necessarily, No waking-creature is asleep, not perpetually but while it is awake." [44]

/10: middle/ And in relation to time, either (11) definitely ([i.e., for a definite period], and this is the *temporal* [proposition], i.e., the one in which /11/ one judges with necessity the continuation of the predicate in the subject, or its denial, not perpetually, but in relation to a definite [or: *specific*] time /12/—as in the statement: " By necessity, every moon is eclipsed, not perpetually but at a time when the earth comes between it and the sun, /13/ and By necessity, no moon is luminous, not perpetually but at this definite time [viz., when it is eclipsed], so Necessarily, something /14/ eclipsed is not luminous, not perpetually, but at this definite time." [45]

Or (12) indefinitely, and this is the temporal *spread* [proposition],

---

[42] The text reads " writing " instead of " moving."

[43] Presumably there is an omission here, and a complete syllogism is intended here as elsewhere. This is then an *EAE*-1 (*Celarent*) syllogism, with both premisses and conclusion uniformly modalized in the mode of temporally restricted necessity characteristic of the general conditional proposition.

[44] The rest of line 9 and the beginning of line 10 gives a (quite out-of-place) restatement of the second premiss. The argument is an *AEE*-2 (*Camestres*) syllogism, with both premisses and conclusion uniformly modalized in the mode of restricted perpetuity characteristic of the special conditional proposition.

[45] This is an *EAO*-3 (*Bokardo*) syllogism, with both premisses and conclusion uniformly modalized in the mode of restricted perpetuity characteristic of the temporal proposition.

/15/ i.e., the one in which one judges with necessity regarding the continuation of the predicate in the subject, or its denial, not perpetually, but in relation /16/ to some [indefinite] times—as in the statement: "Every man exhales, not perpetually but at some [indefinite] times, [and No exhaler inhales not perpetually but at some (indefinite) times—viz., while exhaling],[46] so necessarily No /17/ man inhales, not perpetually but at some [indefinite] time."[47]

Or (13) it is modalized by the modality of the non-necessary, and this is /18/ the *non-necessary existential* [proposition], i.e., the one in which one judges that the continuation of the predicate in the subject, or its denial, is not /19/ by necessity—as in the example: "Every writer is moving, [but] not by absolute necessity; and Some man is a writer, [but] not /20/ by absolute necessity, so consequently, Some men are moving,[48] [but] not by absolute necessity."[49]

Thus the entirety /21/ of [modal] propositions we have distinguished amount to thirteen, namely the general possible, the special possible, the general absolute, /22/ the perpetual, the general conventional, the special conventional, the nonperpetual existential, the absolute necessary, /23/ the general conditional, the special conditional, the temporal, the spread, and the non-necessary existential.

*   *   *

[1072: 17]   *Contradiction*

/18/ Contradiction is the disagreement of two propositions in negation and affirmation so that it is requisite in the nature of the case that /19/ one of them is true and the other false, either (1) determinately (or: *definitely*) as in the necessary and the impossible and the past possible [1073: 1] and the present possible, or (2)

[46] This premiss is evidently missing.

[47] This is an *EAE*-1 (*Celarent*) syllogism, with the minor premiss and the conclusion uniformly modalized in the mode of restricted perpetuity characteristic of the spread proposition.

[48] The text reads: *Some moving [things] are men.*

[49] At this point the printed text (senselessly) adds "by a general absolute." This is an *IAI*-4 (*Dimaris*) syllogism, with both premisses and conclusion uniformly modalized in the mode of non-necessary actuality characteristic of the non-necessary existential proposition.

indeterminately as in the future possible,[50] [for] if one of the pair were definitely determined as having to happen, /2/ then it would be removed from possibility, and the choice would be void. This is as regards to the matter itself; as regards the cause, /3/ further specification is necessary.[51]

*   *   *

/6/   *The Conditions of Contrariety* [52]

/7/ Now if a proposition is special, it suffices for contrariety that (1) [it and its contradictory both] have one [and the same] subject, and (2) that [both] are characterized by one /8/ condition, and (3) one is particular and one universal, and (4) [both have] one predicate, and [both] are characterized by (5) one place and (6) one relation, (7) one power (or: *force*), /9/ (8) one action, and (9) one time.[53] The result of this rule is that if it is to be known that any statement gainsays some other statement, or negates it, /10/ or departs from it, or opposes it, or is such that one is true and the other /11/ false—but are not characterized by the conditions of contradiction—then they are not a pair of contradictories. For example [the requisite of] a single subject: "Zayd /12/ is a clerk," "Zayd is not a clerk": the subject of these two is one and the same, namely Zayd. Also, they comprise one condition, /13/ and are a particular and a universal,[54] and [have] one predicate, and [55] their power (force) is also /14/ one and the same.

/15/ If it (the proposition) is quantitatively-delimited,[56] the

---

[50] This alludes to the problem of future contingency posed in ch. ix of Aristotle's *De Interpretatione*. The position is that future-contingent propositions do indeed have a truth-value of true or false, and thus future-contingent contradictories do indeed contradict one another, but they do not have their truth value (i.e., whatever truth-value they " will turn out to have ") determinately. Cf. N. Rescher, " Truth and Necessity in Temporal Perspective " in R. M. Gale (ed.), *The Philosophy of Time* (New York, 1967).

[51] We omit the (unhelpful) comment on lines 4–5 : overtly an addition by a later commentator.

[52] The printed text reads " The *Eight* Conditions of Contrariety."

[53] This listing appears to result in nine items rather than the eight of the (supplied) heading.

[54] We again omit a brief comment inserted in the printed text at this point.

[55] I suppose *wa* for the *bi* of *bi-'l-quwwa*, as at line 8 above.

[56] That is, has a quantity-indicator (" all " or " some " or " none "). Cf. 816: 3–5 above.

contradictory must also be [definite] in quantity, because two universals may both be false, /16/ as with the statements " Everything is possible," [57] " Nothing is possible "—or two particulars may both be true, /17/ as with the statements " Something is possible," " Something is not possible." But if they differ in quantity, then they must divide /18/ the true and the false, as with the statements " Everything is possible," " Something is not possible."

*   *   *

Since it is impossible [1074: 1] to realize a contradiction except at a single time, and there is difficulty about realizing it, we shall single out each type of proposition /2/ for [separate] discussion.

/3/ As to the general absolute, nothing of its own species contradicts it, because it admits of being non-perpetual,[58] so that with the assumption (or: *supposition*) that /4/ this is the case, this does not realize the irreconcilability of the negative and the affirmative, because of the possibility that there is a time /5/ for one of them that is not a time for the other.[59] But it is requisite to take heed of the link of the prepetual in some of them,[60] because the negative perpetual contradicts /6/ the affirmative, be it perpetual or not; and then, the perpetual may be necessary or not. It is not feasible to regard one /7/ of these two propositions [i.e., the general absolute or the necessary] as the contradictory of this [general] absolute, because it [can be] true that the combination of the [general] absolute together with each of the two propositions /8/ are [both] false when the other part is true. Thus is shown the necessity of heed to the link of perpetuity in /9/ contradicting this [general] absolute.[61]

Even as the general absolute is not contradicted by anything of its

---

[57] Literally not " thing " but " existent," which creates difficulties for the example.

[58] That is, a general absolute cannot be contradicted by another general absolute: thus $(A/\exists t/E![A])$ is not contradicted by $(\sim A/\exists t/E![\sim A])$—but only by the stronger negative absolute perpetual $(\sim A/\forall t/E![\sim A])$.

[59] That is, seemingly opposed general absolutes need not contradict because one may be true at one time and the other at another.

[60] That is, some general absolute propositions may in fact be perpetual. For $(A/\exists t/E![A])$ may, of course, be the case when $(A/\forall t/E![A])$.

[61] That is, the contradictory of the general absolute being the (correspondingly negative) absolute perpetual, it has to be a perpetual proposition.

129

own species, so also the other /10/ propositions are not contradicted by any of their own species, because it [can be] true that the combinations are both false when there is /11/ a true one which differs from them in modality. Rather, that which contradicts them differs from them in quantity and quality /12/ and modality altogether.

/13/ Then know [also] that [modal] propositions are divided into: (1) those which have one part. These are the ones which are subject to a /14/ [single] negation, rather than two conjoint members, such as the general possible, the general absolute, the perpetual, the general conventional, /15/ the necessary absolute, and the general conditional. And (2) those which have two parts. These are the ones which are subject to /16/ two conjoint members, such as the special possible, which is subject to this because of the removal of necessity from both its sides jointly, or /17/ [those which add] a negative member, such as the two [other] specials [62] and the two temporals,[63] and the two actuals (or: *existentials*).[64]

The contradictory of the first division has one part only, /18/ namely what is opposite to it in quantity and quality and modality altogether.[65] But the contradictory of the second division has two parts, namely /19/ [either] (i) what agrees in quantity and is opposite to it in modality, or (ii) is opposite to it in quantity and quality and modality altogether.

* * *

/20/ (1) The contradictory of the general possible is that necessary which is opposite to it in quantity and quality and modality; for example, the statement /21/ " *By necessity*: Some fire is not hot." [66]

(2) The contradictory of the special possible [67] is not of this sort but is the truth of /22/ either the agreeing necessary or the opposite, as

[62] The special conditional and the special conventional.
[63] I.e., the temporal and the spread.
[64] The non-necessary existential and the non-perpetual existential.
[65] The opposites in quantity are universal-particular, in quality affirmative-negative, in modality necessary-possible.
[66] This is to contradict: " *Possibly* : All fire is hot."
[67] The MS (mistakenly) reads: *General possible*. This was, however, treated in the immediately preceding case, beginning with the preceding line.

with the statements: " *By necessity*: Some gold is not meltable " or [1075: 1] " *By necessity*, some of it (gold) is meltable." [68]

(3) The contradictory of the general absolute is [the perpetual] opposite to it, as with the statement "*Perpetually*: Some horse is not neighing."

/2/ (4) The contradictory of [the perpetual] is the general absolute opposite to it, as with the statement: " *With general absoluteness*: Some corporeal-body is not composite."

/3/ (5) The contradictory of the general conventional is its opposite for some times of the description, as with the statement: " *With general absoluteness*: [69] Some animals are not /4/ endowed-with-sensation while they are animals."

(6) The contradictory of the special conventional is, however, not of this sort, but /5/ is the truth of either [the general absolute] which is opposite to it for some times, or the agreeing perpetual; as with the statements: " *With general absoluteness*: Some intoxicants (or: *wines*) /6/ are grapes while they are intoxicants " or [70] " *Perpetually*: Some of them (intoxicants) are not grapes."

(7) The contradictory of the non-perpetual existential /7/ is not of this sort, but is the truth of either the agreeing perpetual or the opposite [perpetual], as with the statement " No man /8/ is laughing actually at all times (or: *perpetually*)," [or: " Some man is laughing actually at all times (or: *perpetually*).] [71]

(8) The contradictory of the absolute necessary is the general possible opposite to it in quantity /9/ and quality, as with the statement: " *By a general possibility*: Some corporeal-body is not moving." [72]

(9) The contradictory of the general conditional /10/ is its opposite for some times of the description, as with the statement: " *By a general possibility*: Some writer does not move while he is a writer." [73]

---

[68] The contradictory of the former being " *By necessity*: All gold is meltable " and of the latter " *Possibly*: Some gold is not meltable."

[69] Presumably the modal prefix should read: *With general conventionality*.

[70] The text (mistakenly) reads *and*, but the logic of the situation requires *or*.

[71] To set aright the logic of the situation, the bracketed addendum must be supplied.

[72] Which contradicts: " *Necessarily*: All corporeal-bodies move."

[73] Which contradicts: " *With conditional generality*: All writers move while they are writers."

/11/ (10) The contradictory of the special conditional is not of this sort, but is the truth of either the opposite, /12/ with the removal of necessity, regarding that specified time, or the agreeing perpetual; as with the statements: " *By a general possibility*: Some moon is not eclipsed /13/ at a time when the earth interposes between it and the sun " or " *Perpetually*: Some of them (some moons) are eclipsed." [74]

(11) The contradictory /14/ of the spread is not of this sort but is the truth of either the opposite, with the removal of necessity, regarding all times, /15/ or the agreeing perpetual; as with the statements: " *It is not necessary that*: Men breathe at any and every time whatsoever," /16/ or " *Perpetually*: Some man breathes."

(12) The contradictory of the non-necessary existential is not of this sort, but is the /17/ truth of either the opposite perpetual, or the agreeing necessary; as with the statements: " *Perpetually*: Some writer does not move " /18/ or [75] " *Necessarily*: Some of them (i.e., some writer) moves." [76]

/19/   *The Syllogism*

/20/ If we infer from one thing toward another, then either that one of them is included in the second, or it is not. Then if /21/ the first is the one of them that is more general then [the other] the more special—or if we infer from the more general to the more special—this is the syllogism. /22/ For example, the inference from a determination for the whole body of the animals—which is more general than man—to its determination for man. /23/ But [77] [the inference] from the particular to the general is induction, for example the inference from a determination of the motion of the lower jaw when /24/ the horse and the ox chew to its determination for animals [generally].

If one of them is not contained in the second, then both of them must be contained in /25/ a [common third], and this is analogy.

[74] At this point number (11), the Temporal, is dropped from the discussion.
[75] The text (mistakenly) reads *and*, but the logic of the situation requires *or*.
[76] The listing goes wrong at two points: (1) It redundantly lists the Necessary and the Necessary Absolute (items 3 and 9), and it omits the Temporal.
[77] I suppose *bal* (but) for *aw* (or).

Consequently, this is as though composed of [both] a syllogism and an induction. [1086: 1] [This is so] because it makes an inference from a determination of the judgment regarding a point of agreement [78] to something connected [with it] through a description shared with it [i.e., a point of similarity], which is the relationship /2/ of induction; and it yields a determination regarding the other part, which is the relationship of syllogism.

/3/ Syllogism is a statement (or: *discourse*) composed of composite statements which, if admitted, necessitate by their nature yet another statement.[79]

The expression /4/ " of [composite] statements " is a precaution against a single premiss because these—like [80] the converse of what follows the converse, and the converse of the contradictory, /5/ and also the falsehood of the contradictory—are not syllogisms.

And by the expression " when admitted " [81] we do not mean that they are to be admitted /6/ in themselves, but that [82] if they were admitted, the conclusion would be necessitated. We mean by " necessity " intellectual necessity, meaning by this that it is a recognition /7/ of the intellect of the two premisses in a special arrangement which necessitates a judgment of the conclusion.

*   *   *

The syllogism is divided /8/ with respect to its form:

(1) Into that in which the conclusion or its contradictory is in fact mentioned. This is the *exceptive* (exclusive) [syllogism]— /9/ as in the statement " If this is a man, then it is an animal," so then if you say " But it is a man " then it follows " that it is an animal." /10/ [Here] this conclusion is such that its overt-declaration was mentioned in the conditional premiss. And if you say " But it is not an animal " it follows then /11/ that " It is not a man." Here this conclusion is different from what was mentioned in that conditional [premiss], but what was mentioned in its contradictory.

[78] Literally: *place of agreement.*
[79] Compare Aristotle, *Anal. Pr.*, 24b18–20.
[80] Read *k* for *b*.
[81] The earlier text reads: " *if* admitted."
[82] The text literally reads: *so that.*

/12/ (2) And [the syllogism is also divided] into that which is not of this sort, and this is the connective [syllogism]—as for example, the statement " Every body is composite and everything composite is created," /13/ from which it follows that " Every body is created." So that [here] neither the conclusion nor its contradictory were mentioned in the syllogism.[83]

(3) Then also, it /14/ is divided according to that of which it is composed [as premises], be they two categoricals, or two disjunctives, or two conjunctives, or a categorical and a conjunctive, /15/ or a categorical and a disjunctive, or a conjunctive and a disjunctive.

(4) And [it is also divided] according to its composition in four figures. For every /16/ one of its judgments [i.e., premises] has two extreme terms, and since the relationship between two of them is an unknown,[84] a thing [linking term] is required which has a relationship to them (the two terms) /17/ in accordance with [the fact that] when we know the two of them (the two premises) we [also] know their relationship to the unknown (conclusion). Now this third [term] must bear to /18/ the two extreme terms (of the conclusion) a known relationship, and because of this it occurs in both premisses,[85] and this third (common term) is called the middle, /19/ since it mediates between the two extreme terms of the conclusion.

*　　*　　*

A syllogism must have two premises and three terms. Let us give a sample /20/ of the categorical [syllogisms]: " All A is B, and All B is C, so All A is C." [86] Two of the terms are the subject of the conclusion /21/ and its predicate. The subject [term of the conclusion] is called *the minor* [term], and the predicate *the major* [term].

[83] This makes it perfectly clear that the categorical syllogism is conceived of as consisting of a pair of premises (only), not as two-premisses-cum-conclusion. This way of regarding the syllogism has far-reaching consequences. Cf. N. Rescher, *Galen and the Syllogism* (Pittsburgh, 1964).

[84] Since otherwise they could not provide a valid basis for relating the two terms of the conclusion.

[85] Note here again the premises-only view of the syllogism, which regards the conclusion as unspecified and unknown.

[86] Note now the shift to an explicit conclusion.

And the premiss which has the minor [term] is the *minor* [*premiss*], /22/ and that which has the major [term] is the *major* [*premiss*]. That [statement] which has the combination of the minor and the major is *the conclusion.*

Now if the middle [term] is predicate in /23/ the minor and subject in the major, this is the first figure, because the natural ordering is present here alone, since /24/ the intellect moves [most naturally] from the subject [term] to the middle, and from it to the predicate.

If the major [premiss] alone is converted [in this natural ordering], then the middle [term] becomes /25/ predicate in both premisses together, and this is the second figure. Likewise, the second figure is reduced to the first [1077: 1] by converting the major.

If the minor [premiss] alone is converted, then the middle [term] becomes subject in both premisses together, and this /2/ is the second figure. It is reduced to the first by converting the minor.

[If the major (premiss) alone is converted, then the middle (term) becomes subject in both premisses together, and this is the third figure. It is reduced to the first by converting the major.] [87] If both premisses are converted together, /3/ the middle term becomes subject in the minor and predicate in the major, and this is the fourth figure. It is very strange /4/ because of the change of both premisses from the natural ordering: the two extreme [terms] fall into the middle, and the middle term into the extremes. [88]

/5/ The four figures have it in common that (1) there is no syllogism from two particulars, (2) nor from two negatives, (3) not from /6/ a negative minor and a particular major, save with the existentials and the special possible. [89]

*   *   *

(The syllogism is divided) /7/ with respect to matter into (1) that

---

[87] This is omitted from the printed text by an error on the part of the scribe— or the printer.

[88] Note the (mild) derogation of the fourth figure. Cf. N. Rescher, *Galen and the Syllogism* (*op. cit.*), p. 10.

[89] Putting the issue of modality aside, these three rules are perfectly correct.

which is composed of two certain-propositions, and this is *demonstration*; and (2) that which is composed of two generally accepted-propositions, /8/ and this is the *topical* [*syllogism*], and (3) that which is composed of two opined-propositions, and this is the *rhetorical* [*syllogism*], and into (4) that which is composed of two [propositions] which [merely] simulate /9/ the true or the accepted or the opined, and this is the *sophistical* [*syllogism*], and (5) into that which is composed of two imagined-propositions, and this is the *poetical* [*syllogism*].[90]

[90] Regarding this classification, which was standard among the Arabic logicians in the time of al-Kindī (b. *ca.* 805), see N. Rescher, *Studies in the History of Arabic Logic* (Pittsburgh, 1963), pp. 30–31, 35–37.

IX

NICHOLAS OF CUSA ON THE QUR'ĀN

A FIFTEENTH-CENTURY ENCOUNTER WITH ISLAM

1. *Preface*

This fall,[1] the 500th anniversary of the death of Nicholas of Cusa —equally well known under the Latinized name of Cusanus—is being commemorated throughout centers of learning in the West. The attention of many minds is focused once more upon the work of this great Catholic thinker who stood on the threshold of that crucial juncture of the Renaissance, separating the medievals from the moderns. Scholar, philosopher, theologian, cardinal, church official, and personal friend to a pope, Nicholas embodied a truly remarkable versatility of capabilities and achievements. On the sky-map of philosophy, his star has gleamed brightly century after century.

It is a sensible view that perhaps the best way to commemorate an important thinker lies in taking serious account of his work, rather than in simply praising it. And since one cannot, within the limits of a single lecture, take into serious account the vast output of a multi-faceted and productive scholar, it becomes necessary to confine oneself to some particular part of his work. I have chosen here to deal with Nicholas of Cusa's treatise on the Qur'ān because to me this treatise seems both to be of considerable interest in itself and to throw some light upon Nicholas' tenor of thought.

2. *Background*

To appreciate the significance of Nicholas of Cusa's work on the Qur'ān, one should begin by looking briefly at the historical back-

[1] Public lecture delivered at the Cusanus Commemoration Conference held at the University of Rochester, 6 November 1964.

ground of the thinking about Islam in the realm of Latin Christianity. This historical course of development may be divided into three (somewhat overlapping) phases.

(*1*) *First Period* (*1100–1250* +). The first period runs from around 1100 to somewhat after 1250. This period saw a great deal of interest in Islam within Latin Christendom. Many scholars occupied themselves with Arabic works, in science and philosophy, and the period was one of active translation of philosophical, scientific, and even theological works from Arabic.

It was during this period that Peter the Venerable, Abbot of Cluny (d. 1156), an able and farsighted scholar and friend of the eminent philosopher Bernard of Clairvaux, sponsored a Latin translation of the Qur'ān. This translation was prepared around 1141–1143 by collaboration between a Spaniard, Hermannus Dalmata, and an Englishman, Robertus Angligena, " Robert the Englishman "—also known as Robertus Retenensis. This version, which " abounds in inaccuracies and misunderstandings, and was inspired by hostile intention," [2] was destined to become the form in which the Qur'ān was known in Latin Christendom. Numerous manuscript copies were made in medieval times, and four centuries later it was published by Theodor Bibliander of Zürich.

During this first period, then, an active and intelligent interest in matters relating to Islam was manifest among European men of learning.

(*2*) *Second Period* (*1250–1400*). The second period runs from roughly 1250 to around 1400. During this period, with the gradual collapse of the Crusades—and the increasing stridency of the Church in keeping crusading fervor aglow in the face of mounting difficulties— a shrill, almost hysterical tone comes into the discussion. One instance, among many, is the *Gesta imperatorum et pontificium* by Thomas of Tuscany (d. 1278). According to Thomas, Muḥammad is a thief, a murderer, a beast in human form, a magician, the firstborn and emissary of Satan himself. [3]

[2] A. J. Arberry, *The Koran Interpreted* (New York, 1955), p. 7.
[3] Nikolaus von Cues, *Sichtung des Alkorans*, tr. by Paul Naumann, 2 vols. (Leipzig, 1943) (*Schriften des Nikolaus von Cues*, ed. E. Hoffman, vols. VI, VII), p. 26 of Preface.

(3) *Third Period (1400–1500)*. The third period runs from about 1400 to around 1500. With the ending of the Crusades and the erosion of the crusading spirit—and the concomitant concentration upon local issues and difficulties—European interest in Islam went into a state of suspension. It was well on the way to atrophy when a development of political history occurred which is of great significance as background for Nicholas' treatise. During the first half of the 15th century, the eyes of thinking European Christians turned once again to the East, focusing upon Constantinople. That great city had slipped by gradual stages into the state of an isolated enclave existing as a beleaguered Christian island within the hostile surrounding sea of the Ottoman Turks. This situation led, on the one hand, to an interest in a possible reconciliation between the Church of Rome and that of the East—a circumstance which took Nicholas himself on a mission to Constantinople in the late 1440's. On the other hand, the Turkish threat to Constantinople rearoused the European interest in Islam which had become dormant since the fervor of the Crusades. The fall of the city in 1453 saw a revival in the Christian polemic against Islam.

Thus, Nicholas of Cusa's treatise on the Qur'ān was part of the reawakening of European concern about Islam which arose in the face of the imminent and ultimately actual fall of Constantinople to the Turks. So much for the historical background.

3. *Sources*

What were Nicholas of Cusa's sources of information about Islam ? We are in the fortunate position of being able to answer this question with great accuracy and detailed exactness. For not only did Nicholas, as a good scholar, cite the sources for his work, but, also, he left his books to the library of the hospital that was endowed by him at Cusa. Here the very books used by him are preserved and his annotations of them can be inspected by interested students.

As to the Qur'ān itself, Nicholas used, as he himself tells us in the preface of his book, the already-mentioned translation sponsored by Peter the Venerable in the 12th century. This translation was unquestionably a mixed asset, for although it did make it possible to have at least *some* first-hand contact with the Qur'ān, its errors and inaccuracies were so numerous and so significant that they rendered the original quite unrecognizable.

Apart from this deficient translation of the Qur'ān itself, Nicholas' most important—and actually more helpful—source, was the treatise entitled *Propugnaculum fidei* by the Florentine Dominican, Ricoldus of Monte Crucis (ca. 1310; printed Venice, 1609).[4] Ricoldus had traveled extensively in the East, and had lived for some years in Baghdad. He knew Arabic and in his book cites the Qur'ān in accurate translations of his own. He is reasonably well informed about Islam, and evinces more factually accurate understanding of Islam than virtually all other medieval writers on the topic. It was in large part from this distinctly superior source that Nicholas' understanding of the nature and teachings of Islam were derived. His own work draws upon that of Ricoldus at virtually every important point.

4. *The Leading Idea*

In 1461–1462, a period during which he held important offices in Rome under the aegis of his friend Pope Pius II, Nicholas of Cusa wrote his *Cribratio Alchorani* (" Sifting of the Qur'ān ").[5] He had been equipped for this task by some personal experience of Islam derived from a visit in Constantinople in 1437–1438, in connection with a mission working in the interests of unity between the Eastern and Western churches. (We might note parenthetically that, in consequence of this, Nicholas himself participated in the negotiations at the Council of Florence in 1438 which resulted in an abortive agreement for such a union.)

Over and above this brief occasion for first-hand contact, Nicholas was widely read in the ramified literature on Islamic matters available in Latin. No contemporary European thinker could match his knowledge of the Latin literature relating to Islamic philosophy and religion.

[4] A particularly useful work for the history of Christian–Muslim relations is Norman Daniel, *Islam and the West: The Making of an Image* (Edinburgh, 1960). See further J. W. Sweetman, *Islam and Christian Theology*, pt. II, vol. I, pp. 116, 160.

[5] Nicholas of Cusa's *Cribratio Alchorani* is now readily accessible in a German translation by Paul Naumann, *op. cit.* Our discussion owes much to Naumann's informative introduction.

The guiding idea of Nicholas' *Cribratio Alchorani* is a shrewd and an interesting one. It is definitely not, as the majority of its medieval predecessors were, a blanket denunciation, but a careful attempt to sift out the Christian and the non-Christian elements of the Qur'ān. (This objective is made explicit in the very title of the treatise itself: *cribrare* = to sift out.) Rather than reject the Qur'ān *en bloc*, Nicholas wants to distinguish between a Muḥammad who has listened to the voice of the God who enters into the hearts of all men, and a Muḥammad who advances ideas and objectives of his own.

Notwithstanding its greater discrimination, Nicholas' *Sifting of the Qur'ān* is avowedly a work of Christian polemic against Islam. Conforming to the tradition derived from St. John of Damascus in the 8th century, who classes Islam as a Christian heresy, Nicholas regards Muḥammad as having started from a Christian position under the influence of Christian (Nestorian) teachers, departing from it at first partly under the corrupting influence of Jews, partly to render the message more readily audible to the heathen Arabs. Then, ultimately, Muḥammad made increasingly radical departures to exploit his growing following as an instrument of personal power.

Inherent in this view is a possibility that greatly intrigued Nicholas and some of his friends. If Islam is a corrupted version of Christianity, if Christianity is the starting point of Islam—the purified proto-Islam of a corrupted Qur'anic Islam—then a Muslim " return " to the Church becomes a thing conceivable. This train of thought provides the background for that very curious document of church history, the letter of 1461–1462 of Pope Pius II to Sultan Muḥammad II calling upon the Sultan to accept Christianity and to become the successor of the Byzantine emperors as temporal head of the Christian Orient.[6] This letter, to which the Sultan did not even deign to make a reply, for a brief time aroused the imagination of Europe by the dazzling prospect of a religious triumph as climax to a long course of military catastrophe in the East.

5. *Nicholas' View of the Qur'ān*

Nicholas of Cusa's conception of the Qur'ān is, as we have

---

[6] See P. Naumann, *op. cit.*, pp. 11–12; cf. Sweetman, *op. cit.*, p. 161, n. 3.

indicated, unique in its radical departure from the standard strain of Christian polemic against Islam. His view is as follows:

Muḥammad's basic impulse was good—his eye was upon the path to God revealed to men imperfectly by Moses and fully by Jesus, and he sought to guide the heathen Arabs to this path and make it easy for them. The Muslim well arose from a sound spring, even though heretical Christians and corrupting Jews poisoned it, and the self-interest which made Muḥammad into a tool of the devil ultimately perverted it.

Not only was Muḥammad's starting intention valid, but the work he produced, the Qur'ān, is of genuine religious merit. It contains much that is sound and incorporates a great deal of truth. It is a work heavily influenced by the Old and New Testaments, whose reflected light illuminates it at many points. (The extent to which this view requires sympathetic interpretation is evidenced by the fact that the Qur'ān contains but one direct quotation from the Scriptures—Qur'ān 21: 105; Ps. 37: 29.) Of course it goes amiss at numerous and crucial junctures, and of course it contains nothing of merit over and above what is to be found in the Gospels. *Si quid pulchri, veri et clari in Alcoran reperitur, necesse est, quod sit radius lucidissimi Evangelii* (*Cribratio*, I, 6).

How did Nicholas explain his view that Muḥammad, having caught many glimpses of Christian truths, went fundamentally astray? How did he account for the departures of the Qur'ān from the New Testament? Here Nicholas has ready a threefold answer: (1) misunderstandings due to the impeding machinations of Nestorians and of Jews who influenced Muḥammad, (2) deliberate didactic departures to adapt the message to the primitive and pagan Arabs, and (3) deliberate falsifications to serve the self-interest of the Prophet and/or the political advantage of his following.

The greater part of Nicholas of Cusa's discussion is thus devoted to a detailed critique of the departures of the Qur'ān from Christian teachings and the deployment of a Christian polemic—in its fundamentals along the usual lines—against the teachings of Islam, dwelling largely upon an apology of those Christian teachings which, like the doctrine of the trinity, had formed the foci of Islamic attacks on Christianity.

On Nicholas' view of the matter, the Qur'ān is thus a mixture in which the sound grains of truth are intermingled with the chaff of falsity. The correct Christian approach to the Bible of Islam cannot be a complete condemnation, but should be a carefully discriminative sifting (*cribratio*) of truth from error.

This attitude infuses and shapes the whole strategy of Nicholas' polemic against Islam. It is entirely *internal*, taking its stand upon the Qur'ān itself: upon its own recognition of the truth of the Gospels. As Nicholas sees the matter, the Qur'ān, in its recognition of the Bible and in the acceptance of the Biblical view of Jesus' message and role, condemns itself out of its own mouth at all points at which it departs from Biblical teachings. This line of thought determined Nicholas' concept of the basis for a sound and effective Christian polemic against Islam, and led him to dwell at some length upon matters in respect to which the declarations of the Qur'ān appeared to him as self-contradictory. (One example is ch. 9 of Bk. III, devoted to the thesis "that Muhammad wrote of Christ sometimes as god and man both, sometimes only as man, and sometimes as god in the singular, sometimes in the plural.")

This point of view also provides the rationale which brought Nicholas to that favorite concept of our day: the idea of a dialogue. Writing to his friend John of Segovia, he welcomed the idea of a conference with the Muslims: *Non est dubium medio principium temporalium, quos Teucri sacerdotibus praeferunt, ad colloquia posse perveniri, et ex illis furor mitigabitur, et veritas se ipsam ostendet cum profectu fidei nostrae.* In this hopeful view of the constructive value of a " dialogue " (colloquium)—that this would mitigate the furor of disputation and prove useful for religion—Nicholas of Cusa is perhaps more a child of our time than of his own.

6. *Some Blind Spots of Nicholas' View of the Qur'ān*

It is, however, only just to say that—despite the fact that his judgment of the Qur'ān was unusually favorable for his place and time—Nicholas' view of the Bible of Islam was subject to certain sharp limitations, perhaps even deserving the name of blind spots.

Of these, the first and most obvious relates to the literary quality of the Qur'ān. The Bible of Islam is a work whose beauty of language was from the first accepted by Muslims as a proof of divine inspiration. This element was, of course, wholly lost on Nicholas, for whom the Qur'ān (seen only in dry-as-dust translations) might as well have been a dissertation of scholastic theology.

A more crucial point is bound up with this first blind spot. Nicholas is able to see merit in the Qur'ān only at those points at which it agrees with the Gospels. He is flatly unwilling to grant that there may be some special merit of insight or inspiration in the Scripturally nonredundant parts of the Qur'ān—not, to be sure, as regards its declarations on matters of faith and doctrine, but in its essentially secular ordinances, for example, those regarding the reformation of the social or communal affairs of the Arabs.

In his eagerness to use the Qur'ān itself as an instrument of his cause, Nicholas is occasionally led to do (no doubt unwittingly) violence to the text in order to bend it to his objectives. Consider, for example, the following Qur'ānic passage, cited in the translation of A. J. Arberry: (Sūrah 4, " Women," verses 167–170):

> People of the Book, go not beyond the bound in your religion, and say not as to God but the truth. The Messiah, Jesus son of Mary, was only the Messenger of God, and His Word that He committed to Mary, and a Spirit from Him. So believe in God and His Messengers, and say not, " Three." Refrain; better is it for you. God is only One God. Glory be to Him—that He should have a son! To Him belongs all that is in the heavens and in the earth; God suffices for a guardian. The Messiah will not disdain to be a servant of God, neither the angels who are near stationed to Him.[7]

This is an obvious piece of anti-Christian, anti-trinitarian polemic. But Nicholas cites only a part of the text in isolation from its context: " Jesus son of Mary is God's messenger (*sic*, there is no ' only ') and His spirit (*sic*, and not ' a spirit from Him ') and His word sent unto Mary " (*Cribratio*, I, 12). Taken thus, out of context and in deceptive translation, Nicholas (*loc. cit.*) uses this passage as a proof text to show that the Qur'ān itself countenances a trinitarian position and recognizes the divinity of Jesus.

---

[7] The best English translation of the Qur'ān is that of A. J. Arberry, *The Koran Interpreted*, 2 vols. (London, 1955). Arberry's preface provides interesting information about the transmission of the Qur'ān to Europe.

Needless to say, however, there should be no astonishment over the fact that the merits which Nicholas can find in the Qur'ān extend over a limited area. The noteworthy thing is that there is any such area at all.

7. *The Rationale of Nicholas' Treatise*

The unique character of Nicholas' treatise, as a Christian evaluation of the Qur'ān that is prepared to find in it good points as well as bad, derives not from his sources—how could it?—but from his own brain. It developed against the backdrop of his thinking about the nature of religion as such.

Nicholas' attitude toward the nature and diversity of religions is set forth in his important treatise " On Peace or Concord in Religion " (*De pace seu concordantia fidei*): [8] Here Nicholas expounds a view of religions which—while not (of course) overtly relativistic—emanates a certain aura of relativism. The basic concept developed here may be indicated by the analogy of mountain climbing. The mountaintop represents the summit of genuine religious knowledge, and the different paths leading up to the same summit—some rendering its attainment easy of access, others rocky, difficult, and full of pitfalls—represent various diverse religions. The analogy—which I use only for explanatory purposes: it is nowhere explicit in Nicholas' writings—illustrates graphically the tenor of his thought about religious diversity, a diversity he regards as perfectly legitimate—if not as regards the fundamental of doctrine, then at any rate as regards rite. *Una religio in rituum varietate.* The positivity of Nicholas' approach to the Qur'ān must be judged—and can only be understood—within this background context of the basic rationale of his religious philosophy. The comprehensive philosophical perspective he brought to the particular case made it possible for Nicholas to see gleams of the light of Truth where eyes of narrower vision saw only the unmixed handwork of the devil.

8. *Conclusion*

We live in an era which, whatever may be its shortcomings in

[8] See further R. Klibansky and H. Bascour, *Nicolai de Cusa de Pace Fidei*, Supp. III of *Mediaeval and Renaissance Studies*, The Warburg Institute, University of London (London, 1956).

other respects, is a time of increased mutual sympathy and under-standing between diverse religious groups. In a domain once ruled by bitter theological warfare, we can hear the beating of the wings of the dove of peace. The idea of a reconciliation between Christianity and Islam may even nowadays seem remote, but it cannot today be dismissed as an utter absurdity. The thesis of St. John of Damascus that Islam is but a Christian heresy provides the continuing basis for a possible reconciliation, at any rate on the Christian side of the divide. Nicholas of Cusa realized, more clearly than any other theologian of his day, the implications, both theo-logical and practical, of such a position. Ours is a generation preoccupied almost to obsession with the concept of communication. The phrase "lack of communication" has become one of the hallmark clichés of our day. In his stress upon the need for Christian-Islamic interchange, Nicholas struck a note that evokes resonance in our thoughts. As Christianity and Islam draw increasingly into peaceful contact with one another in our own time, Nicholas of Cusa deserves more and more clearly to be numbered as a member of the small band of men of prophetic insight. And come what may, one cannot but honor him not only as a mind of great penetration, but as a man of good will, whose sympathetic vision was able to discern the light of truth where his compatriots saw nothing except the unmixed blackness of error.

X

THE IMPACT OF ARABIC PHILOSOPHY ON THE WEST

Consider the following hypothetical account. It is not a quotation, but purely a "straw man." None the less it would, I feel sure, receive widespread assent:

> From the late 8th century there arose such a thing as a characteristically Arabic philosophy. Interest in this developed rapidly in the Latin-speaking orbit in the wake of the Islamic explosion across the Mediterranean world. It came to a head in the substantial array of 12th- and 13th-century Latin translations, which led to widespread attention to the Arabic philosophers. Afterwards, with the increase of anti-Islamic feeling in the wake of the crusades, and the condemnations of " Averroism " by the Church during the 13th century, European interest in Arabic philosophy came to a halt. There was then a gap of almost half a millennium and the influence of Arabic philosophy in the West was not to resume until the rise of Arabistic scholarship in Europe in the 18th century.

This account of the matter is shot through with mistakes from beginning to end and might be called the " intelligent man's bundle of errors " regarding this phase of cultural history. My objective here is to delineate a picture—a picture to be drawn with admittedly broad brushstrokes—that gives a more accurate portraiture of the facts.

I shall begin by sawing off the limb represented by the very title of my paper. The very notion of an *Arabic Philosophy* is without tenable credentials. In so far as a very concise summary of a very complex matter can ever be correct it is a warranted thesis that *there is no such thing as an Arabic philosophy* (just as it would be true to say that there is no such thing as an Arabic geometry). By a complex process of transmission—which I shall not even attempt to describe here—the

147

Arabic-speaking peoples (including not only Arabs, but Syrian Christians, Persians, Turks, and others) took hold of and assimilated Greek philosophy, primarily that of Aristotle and his later commentators and expositors, just as they took over Euclidean geometry. They carried forward and developed the Greek ideas, discussions, and controversies. The chess board and the pieces are old and Greek, even if some of the moves are new. The work of the Arabic-using philosophers of the Middle Ages deserves the title of " Arabic philosophy " in about the same sense that the work of the German Shakespeare scholars of the 19th century deserves the title of " German literature." Arabic philosophy has nothing to do with " oriental wisdom "—it is *Greek philosophy carried forward in an Arabic-language setting.* It is in *this* sense that the term is to be understood throughout our subsequent discussion.

This fact is of the utmost importance for our topic of " The Impact of Arabian Philosophy on the West." It shows that this issue comes down to something quite different: The role of Arabic philosophical writings in the recovery of Greek philosophy and science in Latin-using Europe. In putting the matter in this way I am, of course, construing " Philosophy " in its academic technical sense, excluding that all-too-familiar usage that permits one to speak of a " philosophy of automobile salesmanship." If I were to broaden the topic, its most plausible expansion would be into the area of Islamic religion, which exercised an extensive and profound influence upon Christian apologetics in the Middle Ages (for example, in giving to the conception of the Trinity an enormous—and perhaps even undue—prominence). I want, however, to resist any such broadening of the topic: it is quite large enough as it is.

It is entirely wrong to think there was any significant degree of interest in Europe in matters Arabic or Islamic before 1100. An authority reports that before that year he was able to find only one single mention of the name of Mahomet in medieval literature outside Spain and southern Italy.[1] But in 1095 came the first crusade, and in its wake there arose throughout Europe a great surge of interest in matters Arabic and Islamic. From 1120 onward, everyone in

[1] R. W. Southern, *Western Views of Islam in the Middle Ages* (Cambridge, Mass., 1962), p. 28.

Europe had some picture of what Islam meant, and possessed some information—or misinformation—about the state of things in the Arabic-speaking world. In particular, an active interest in Arabic work in philosophy and in the sciences arose and rapidly diffused itself throughout the community of scholars. Spain and especially Sicily—where the Norman kingdom provided the locus of peaceful contact between European, Byzantine, and Arabic scholars— provided the centers of translation and transmission from which Arabic work became diffused throughout Europe.

What sorts of materials did Latin Europe take over from the Arabs in the 12th and 13th centuries? The answer is simple and at first sight perhaps somewhat surprising: the only things to be taken over were materials relating to Greek mathematics, science, and philo- sophy—and the Arabic development thereof. The process of transmission was thus a highly selective one. Arabic works in literature, history, legal theory, and theology were not touched by the translators: the patrons who sponsored translations had no interest in them. The Medieval Latins did indeed take over more than 100 significant scholarly works from the Arabs—but essentially all of it was work that extended or deepened their grasp of Greek learning. It is, I believe, correct to say that Qur'ān is the only Arabic work of a strictly Islamic (non-Greek) character to have been translated by scholars into a European language before modern times.

Throughout the Middle Ages, European interest in the vast corpus of Arabic learning was never focused on any strictly Arabian ideas or contributions as such—the Arabic writings were simply an instrument, a telescope through which the truths in the sciences inherited from antiquity could be discerned. Alkindi (b. c. 805), who created an Arabic home for Greek natural science; Alfarabi (b. c. 873), who did the same for Aristotelian logic; Avicenna (b. 980), who offset Aristotle's primacy with ideas drawn from Galen and the Stoics; and the great Averroes (b. 1126), a more royalist Aristotelian than King Aristotle himself—these were the "Arabic thinkers" in whom the Latin medievals took interest.

The great revival of learning in Europe which began to flower in the 12th century, feeding on the fuel of translations from the Arabic, went off on its own course. The distaste for things Mohammedan that came about as the crusades dragged along, and the Church's hostility to Averroism, impeded intellectual contact and active preoccupation with material of Islamic provenience. And anyhow, the *accessible* Arabic material that resonated to European interests had been pretty well exhausted. By about 1300 the processes of active translation had slowed down to a mere trickle.

But this was not so with the processes of diffusion! The Latin translations from the Arabic continued to be copied, circulated, and studied. And the great names of the major Arabic scientists, and also of the great men of Arabic philosophy—Alkindi, Alfarabi, and Avicenna—continued to flow from the pens of medieval scholars. In the *Divine Comedy* Dante (whose indebtedness to Moslem traditions has been established in many respects)consigns Muḥammad to one of the lower hells together with other " sowers of scandals and schism." But Avicenna and Averroes enjoy the benefits of somewhat more comfortable billeting in Purgatory. Throughout the 14th and early 15th centuries the influence of Arabic philosophical writings in Europe continued steadily, but slowly—on a greatly diminished scale. The *raison d'être* for an oblique approach to ancient philosophy was eroding away as the ancient writings became increasingly available, and new, indigenously European work was produced on such a vast scale as to put the material of Arabic provenience more and more into the shade.

With the Renaissance, however, there occurred a highly significant (and yet relatively neglected) revival in Western recourse to Arabic philosophical work. We commonly—and justly—think of the Renaissance in terms of two major phenomena: (1) a turning away from the work of the medievals and back to that of the ancients themselves, and (2) a turning away from the authority of Aristotle— the prime authority of the Medievals—to that of other ancient authorities, especially Plato and the Pythagoreans. But a third quite importantphenomenonisoverlooked bythisoversimplifiedpicture:the Renaissance is also a time of renewed influence of Arabic philosophy.

During the first half of the 15th century the eyes of thinking European Christians turned to the East—focusing upon Constantinople. This great city had slipped by gradual stages into the state of an isolated enclave existing as a beleaguered Christian island within the hostile surrounding sea of the Ottoman Turks. This situation led, on the one hand, to an interest in a possible reconciliation between the Church of Rome and that of the East—a circumstance which took Nicholas of Cusa on a mission to Constantinople in the late 1440's. On the other hand, the Turkish threat to Constantinople re-aroused the European interest in matters Arabic and Islamic, which had become dormant since the fever-pitch of the early Crusades. The fall of the city in 1453 presaged: (1) a great revival in the Christian polemic against Islam; (2) the revival of interest in the ancients; and (3) the renewal of interest in the Arabic philosophers as continuators of the work of the ancients.

To trace developments of interest to us we must go back a bit in the chronology to the Norman Kingdom in Sicily and southern Italy in the 13th century. The emperor Frederic II of Hohenstauffen (1215–1250)—one of the Christian " sultans of Sicily " whose personal and official life at the court of Palermo was very much in the oriental style (dressing in the Eastern manner, maintaining a harem, etc.) [2]—had founded the University of Naples in 1224, the first in Europe to be established by a definite charter. In the curriculum of this university—whose pupils included St. Thomas Aquinas—the works of Aristotle and his Arabic expositors played an important role. The university exerted an influence on others throughout Europe, but especially on two other Italian universities, those of Bologna and Padua. These institutions in the (ultimately) Venetian orbit of northern Italy continued throughout the Middle Ages as hotbeds of " Averroism ": i.e., the study of Aristotle in a faithful, authentic, unchristianized manner. And such scholastic doctors as Urbanus of Bologna, Paul of Venice (d. 1428), and Cajetanus of Thienis (1387–1465) kept up the authority of Averroes into the Renaissance. And the disputes between Pietro Pomponazzi and Augustino Nifo inaugurated around 1500 a new and brilliant epoch for the Averroism of Padua and Bologna. The drive to get back to authentic Aristotelianism got under way: in 1497 the Greek text of Aristotle was for the first time expounded at Padua.

In this context, the renewed interest in the East coming in the wake

[2] See P. K. Hitti, *History of the Arabs* (6th ed., Princeton, 1956), ch. 42.

of the decline and fall of Constantinople led—primarily at Padua and Bologna—to a restored interest in the Arabic expositions of Aristotle, to a renewal of " Averroism." What had begun with the subtle disputes of the scholastic doctors of Paris came to bear fruit among the materialistic teachers of the medical schools and the sceptical men of the world in the cities of northern Italy. The patricians of Venice and the lecturers of Padua made Averroism the hallmark of advanced and enlightened thinking.

We consequently come now to a second wave of Latin translations of Arabic philosophical works: this time confined wholly to Italy. The translation of Andreas Alpagus (d. 1520)—primarily of medical works of Avicenna—were made directly from the Arabic by a Padua professor who had spent over thirty years in the East in the study of Arabic and the pursuit of Avicenna manuscripts. More prominent are the translators Elia del Medigo (fl. c. 1490), and Jacob Mantinus (d. 1549), who dealt primarily with Avicenna and Averroes. These last two were typical of the work of this Renaissance period in that their Latin translations were made—not from the original Arabic, but from Hebrew versions, made in the Middle Ages by Spanish Jews. In this regard we must note the cultural significance of the ending of the toleration of the Jews in Spain in the days of Ferdinand and Isabella, transplanting Jewish scholars from Spain to Italy, where a receptive environment existed for the latinization of the hebraized Muslim learning they had brought from Spain.

This " second wave " in the latinization of Arabic philosophy led to a curious and ironic circumstance. The Italian Aristotelians of the period—typified at the highest point of development by Julius Caesar Scaliger and Jacob Zabarella—now possessed a detailed and accurate understanding of Aristotle's philosophical system vastly in excess of anything heretofore known in Latin Europe. At the same time, on the other hand, the impact of anti-Aristotelianism—typified at its most acute point of development by Peter Ramus (1515– c. 1560)—exhibited not only a force and vehemence but also an influence heretofore unprecedented. Thus at the very juncture when the sympathetic understanding of Aristotle came to a head, so also did the hostile and critical opposition that led to his dethronement as a prime authority in philosophy.

However, one must not be tempted, in the face of the fact that Renaissance Aristotelianism was pretty much a " lost cause," to put the second wave of influence of Arabic philosophy on the shelf to gather dust as one of the futilities of history. The Averroist tradition of Padua kept alive the Arabic interest in and spirit of inquiry respecting natural science, until the time that it provided intellectual grist to the mill of Galileo and his teachers. And this admittedly indirect contribution of importantly contributing to the school of natural philosophy that nurtured Galileo may surely be counted as one of the most significant facets of the " Impact of Arabian Philosophy on the West." By this route Arabic philosophy helped to provide for the intellectual pressure-cooker of northern Italy in the Renaissance one of those fuels of controversy that first fed the fires of the modern sciences of nature.

I come finally to the third and perhaps least well-known wave of Arabic influence upon Western thought before the strictly modern phase of Islamic studies: its impingement upon Protestant scholars in the 17th century. It is, of course, a well-known general phenomenon that Protestant theological doctrine sought to compensate for loss of stability in the authority of the church by turning to the authority of scripture, and that as a result a strong impetus was given to Biblical scholarship in the Protestant orbit. This line of influence gave a definite impetus to Arabic scholarship in Europe as an adjunct to the study of Biblical antiquity. Some of the instances of this phenomenon are well known—for example, the influential activity of Joseph Justus Scaliger (1540–1609) at Leiden, and the inauguration by Archbishop William Laud of an Arabic professorship at Oxford in 1636, to rival the Cambridge professorship endowed by Sir Thomas Adams four years earlier. The motives which animated Adams, later Lord Mayor and still later a prisoner in the Tower, are well summed up in a letter sent to him on 9 May 1636 by the Vice-Chancellor of Cambridge.

To our very loving and much respected friend Mr. Thomas Adams att his howse in Gracious Street in London.

Worthy Sir,
Having these foure yeares enjoyed your bountifull exhibition for the maintenaunce of a Professor of the Arabick tongue in our University,

and now also understanding your pious desire of setling it for perpetuity; wee cannot but returne yow the Scholars tribute of thanks and honor due to so noble a Benefactor, and shall upon any intimation from yow be ready to serve yow with our best counsells and endeavors for the improving it to those good ends to which yow intend it. The worke it selfe wee conceive to tend not onely to the advancement of good Literature by bringing to light much knowledge which as yet is lockt upp in that learned tongue; but also to the good service of the King and State in our commerce with those Easterne nations, and in Gods good time to the enlarging of the borders of the Church, and propagation of Christian religion to them who now sitt in darkness. . . . God prosper the worke according to your pious intentions; and render a full reward of it to yow and yours; making your memory as the memories of all other our famous Benefactors, ever precious among Us! [3]

Less well known than it should be is the linkage between this " third wave " of Arabic influence and the preceding (second wave) Averroism of Bologna and Padua.

The linkage is most sharply illustrated by the Scaliger family. Scaliger *père*, Julius Caesar Scaliger (1484–1558), educated at both Bolgna and Padua, represents the " Averroism " of these institutions toward the zenith of its development. He was to Aristotle's *Physics* what Zabarella was to his *Logic*: both Leibniz and Sir William Hamilton recognize him as the best modern exponent of the physics and metaphysics of Aristotle. Scaliger *fils*, Joseph Justus Scaliger (1540–1609), was educated by his father and also studied at Paris. He attained very substantial competence in both Hebrew and Arabic and on the basis of his knowledge of these—in addition to classical—sources, he revolutionized the study of ancient chronology. A modern classical scholar of no mean credentials unqualifiedly calls Scaliger " The greatest scholar of modern times." [4] A Protestant convert, Scaliger took up an influential professorship at Leiden, when he patronized and encouraged Hugo Grotius.

Let us now turn to a second remarkable father–son combination. Edward Pocock, the elder (1604–1691), after training at Oxford stayed for five to six years at Aleppo and then for three years at Constantinople. Perhaps the finest British Arabist until Lane in the 19th century, Pocock became the first incumbent of Laud's Arabic

---

[3] Quoted from A. J. Arberry, *Oriental Essays* (London, 1960), pp. 12–13.
[4] Richard Copley Christie in the 11th ed. of the *Encyclopaedia Britannica*.

professorship at Oxford in 1636. A good friend of Grotius, his remarkable record includes not only important editions and Latin translations of Arabic texts, but even an Arabic translation of Grotius' treatise *De Veritate* (publ. in 1660).

The son, Edward Pocock the younger (1648–1727), produced (*inter alia*) two important works: a Latin translation of 'Abd al-Laṭīf's *Description of Egypt* and one of Ibn Ṭufail's *Ḥayy ibn Yaqẓān* (under the title " The Self-taught Philosopher ": *Philosophus autodidactus*), published in 1671 from the Arabic text edited by his father. From the standpoint of Arabic influence on the West, this second work calls for at least a brief discussion.

Ḥayy ibn Yaqẓān (" the living one " + man, " son of the Vigilant " + God) is a philosophical romance based on a rough model by Avicenna. Its hero grows up alone on a desert island and comes to develop out of his own head—by natural rather than revealed illumination—the essentials of Aristotelian knowledge and Islamic religion. The guiding concept is that human capacity—unaided by any external inspiration—may attain to the higher knowledge of the world and discover by degrees its dependence on a Supreme Being.

After its Latin translation by Pocock the younger (1671) the tale enjoyed virtually a sensation in Protestant Europe (translated into Dutch, 1672; English, 1674; German, 1726). It exerted a substantial theological influence on some of the more quietistic English sects—especially the Quakers. The first English translation (1674) was that of the important Quaker schismatic, George Keith. Arrested by the similarity of Ibn Ṭufail's views to his own, Keith, though innocent of Arabic, immediately set about putting Pocock's labored Latin into noble English; his version, annotated in the spirit of Quakerism, appeared in 1674. Keith observed that the infidel author " hath been a good man, and far beyond many who have the name of Christians "—a striking contrast to the prevailing intolerance towards Islam!—and added that he " showeth excellently how far the knowledge of a man, whose eyes are spiritually opened, differeth from that knowledge that men acquire simply by hearsay or reading." Barclay seized upon the unexpected revelation from the East in his *Apology for the True Christian Divinity*, first published in 1678:

There is a book translated out of the Arabick, which gives an account of one Hai Ebn Yakdhan, who, without converse of man, living in an island alone, attained to such a profound knowledge of God, as to have immediate converse with him, and to affirm that the best and most certain knowledge of God is not that which is attained by premises promised, and conclusions deduced, but that which is enjoyed by conjunction of the mind of man with the Supreme Intellect after the mind is purified from its corruptions, and is separated from all bodily images, and is gathered into a profound stillness.[5]

There seems to be good reason for regarding this tale as one of the inspirations for *Robinson Crusoe*; Defoe's model was an anonymous Crusoe-type story printed in London in 1761 entitled *The Life and Surprising Adventures of Don Antonio de Trezzanio*, much of which is extracted or paraphrased from Simon Ockley's version of *Hayy ibn Yaqzān*. This affords what is surely one of the most curious of the " curiosities of literature." One cannot but wonder how it would have struck Avicenna that one of his minor philosophical tracts should prove the precursor of one of the great classics of adolescent literature!

I do not want to leave the impression that the Scaliger–Pocock foray into Arabic philosophy was an isolated phenomenon. It fostered interest and stirred up activity. I shall cite just one of the more interesting instances, Pierre Vattier (1623–1667). A man of far-ranging interests and curious learning—a great admirer of Avicenna—personal physician to the Duke of Orleans—Vattier was an energetic Arabist, who filled the chair in Arabic at the Collège de France with distinction. His Latin translation of a logic treatise of Avicenna's (Paris, 1658) is—along with the work of the elder Pocock—one of the earlier milestones of European Arabistic scholarship.

In reaching the end of my tale, let me pause for a brief summary. Our discussion has tried to show that the influence of Arabian philosophy on the West made its impact in three major " waves ":

(1) In the 12th and 13th centuries, the first period of European impingement, Arabic philosophical writings exerted a significant stimulative influence on the great synthesis of Christian Aristotelianism by St. Albert the Great and St. Thomas Aquinas.

[5] Quoted from A. J. Arberry, *op. cit.*, p. 21.

156

(2) In the Italian Renaissance of the 15th to mid-16th centuries, Averroism exerted a great influence in the study of the philosophy of nature at Padua and Bologna, with the result that Arabic philosophy was operative as a significant force in the intellectual ferment that underlay the work of Galileo and saw the beginnings of modern science.

(3) In the late 16th and 17th centuries the study of Arabic philosophy contributed to a small but significant extent to the intellectual ferment of European Protestantism—with various results, of which one of the most striking is that in one significant instance Arabic philosophy served as a stimulus to the philosophico-religious ideology of English pietism.

Thus, in closing, it seems fair to terminate our discussion of " The Impact of Arabian Philosophy on the West " with the observation that this influence has not only been extensive and profound, but relatively continuous and astonishingly diversified.[6]

[6] Public lecture given at De Paul University on 15 May, 1965.

INDEX

This is an *Index of Names* only. In the alphabetic ordering of Arabic names, the prefixes *al-*, *ibn*, and *abū* have been ignored.